A BRIEF GUIDE
TO SOURCES OF
FIBER AND TEXTILE INFORMATION

By Helen G. Sommar
Manager, Technical Information Center
Celanese Fibers Company

I**R**P Information Resources Press
Washington, D.C.   1973

Available from
Information Resources Press
2100 M Street, N.W.
Washington, D.C. 20037

Library of Congress Catalog Card Number 72-89909
ISBN 0-87815-009-9

Preface

This is one of many guides to scientific and technical information sources in specific subject areas which are scheduled to follow Saul Herner's more general book, *A Brief Guide to Sources of Scientific and Technical Information*. Information related to fibers and textiles is found in the literature of organic, inorganic, and physical chemistry; physics; chemical and mechanical engineering; agriculture; and polymer science, among others; as well as in the more obvious sources of fiber science and textile technology. To minimize overlap with other books in this series, I have tried to limit the contents of this *Brief Guide* to those sources which focus specifically on fibers and textiles or which contain a significant proportion of material pertaining to these subjects. Moreover, since this series is intended to cover only scientific and technical information, sources of business and commercial textile information have been excluded.

In the past five to ten years, changes in textile information sources have been frequent and far-reaching in scope. New textile journals have appeared, and others have been discontinued. Many journals have begun printing abstracts with each article, and a few now provide keyterms for each article as well. Two textile thesauri have been published. New textile information services have come into existence, and sophisticated information retrieval systems have become available. Consequently, I have excluded from the appropriate chapters many source guides, handbooks, dictionaries, classification schemes, and

iii

similar material published before 1960, particularly when more recent substitutes exist. As a result of rapid developments in textile information sources, there may be some changes made in publications, services, or prices described in this book before it reaches print. However, I have attempted to provide the most current information possible under the circumstances.

In a *Brief Guide* such as this, it is impossible to include every relevant source of information available throughout the world. In some chapters, I have given only typical examples of some information sources, such as annual reports which include information on current research and standards publications. In other chapters—for example, those covering source guides and retrospective searching services—I have tried to include every appropriate information source.

No deliberate attempt has been made to exclude information sources provided in foreign languages or based in countries other than the United States. However, the emphasis of this *Brief Guide* is clearly on English-language sources and, in some areas, on services available in the United States.

Many individuals and organizations have given me considerable help in collecting the material for this book. In particular, I want to thank Darlene Ball of Burlington Industries, Jim Baker of the School of Textiles Library at North Carolina State University, Ron Richardson of Allied Chemical Corp., and many other members of the Textile Information Users Council. I also appreciate the excellent cooperation of representatives of the organizations which provide information services described in this book. Mary Richardson is also due my thanks for typing the manuscript. Finally, I am grateful to Stanley Backer of MIT and P. H. Cannon, my supervisor, for their confidence and encouragement.

Charlotte, N.C.
June 1972

Contents

Illustrations

Acknowledgements

Cover Photo: "Yarn Processing"; Courtesy of the American Textile Manufacturers Association, Washington, D.C.

Figure 1 is reprinted from the *Alerting Bulletin* of the *Textiles; Paper* section of *Central Patents Index* by kind permission of Derwent Publications Ltd. Figures 2 and 3, reprinted from CA Condensates, and Figure 4, reprinted from *Chemical Titles,* are used by kind permission of the Chemical Abstracts Service, a division of the American Chemical Society. Figure 5 is reprinted from the *Uniterm Index to U.S. Chemical and Chemically Related Patents* by kind permission of IFI/Plenum Data Corporation. Figure 6 is reprinted from *Keyterm Index* by kind permission of *Textile Technology Digest* of the Institute of Textile Technology. Figure 10 is reprinted from the *Journal of the Textile Institute* and the *Textile Research Journal* by kind permission of The Textile Institute, Manchester, England, and the Textile Research Institute, Princeton, New Jersey, respectively. Figure 11 is reprinted from the *Bulletin de l'Institut Textile de France* by kind permission of l'Institut Textile de France. Figure 12 is reprinted from the Key Term Index by kind permission of *Textile Chemist and Colorist* of the American Association of Textile Chemists and Colorists.

1

Information Directories and Source Guidance

In information science parlance, sources of information are categorized as primary, secondary, and tertiary. Primary sources include monographs, reports, papers, and articles which report the results of original research and development investigations. Secondary sources are compendia based on primary sources and include textbooks, encyclopedias, abstracting and indexing services, and review publications. Tertiary sources are compilations of primary *and* secondary sources. Therefore, they list the inventory of, and the means of access to, a vast storehouse of information. These assets, coupled with the belief that one can never have too many tertiary sources, lead to the subject of this chapter—tertiary sources of information on textiles and fibers.

The sources listed here are of many types. They include conventional bibliographies of books and journals and information directories which provide lists of books, primary journals, and abstract publications. The less conventional publications include directories of information centers, abstracting services, research laboratories, and associa-

1

tions through which data may be obtained, as well as journals that announce scientific and technical meetings which often are sources of unpublished information. Finally, there is the unique National Referral Center for Science and Technology, which directs the person requiring specialized information to organizations that may be able to provide it.

In addition to the sources outlined in this chapter, the lists of publications covered by *Textile Technology Digest* and *World Textile Abstracts,* which both publish in their first issues each year, can also be considered tertiary sources.

A1 **ABSTRACTING SERVICES   Vol. 1—Science and Technology** The Hague, Netherlands, Federation Internationale de Documentation, 1969. $10. From: National Federation of Science Abstracting and Indexing Services, 2102 Arch St., Philadelphia, Pa., 19103.

Information given for each abstracting service includes editorial staff; subject and source coverage; number of abstracts published; frequency of publication of abstracting service and indexes; arrangement of abstracts; related magnetic tape, Selective Dissemination of Information (SDI),* and other services; subscription cost; and other pertinent data. Volume 1 lists approximately 1,300 abstracting journals and other periodicals which publish significant numbers of abstracts. Included are approximately 30 abstracting services related to fibers and textiles.

A2 **BIBLIOGRAPHY OF TEXTILE BOOKS** New York, Committee on Textile Education, American Association of Textile Technologists, Inc., 1968. Textile Technology Monograph No. 104. $1 to AATT members, $2 to nonmembers. From: American Association of Textile Technologists, Inc., 620 Fifth Ave., New York, N.Y. 10019.

*An SDI service is one that will store a "profile" describing the interests of an individual or group of individuals and will match this profile against newly published literature, usually by computer, on a regular basis. When a new publication appears to match the interests of a particular individual, the publication is listed and brought to his attention.

A classified list of more than 200 books, including encyclopedias, handbooks, and dictionaries, selected from both recent publications and older sources of information that have current value. The *Bibliography* also lists addresses of publishers of textile literature and of textile associations that provide current information.

A3 **DIRECTORY OF INFORMATION RESOURCES IN THE UNITED STATES** Library of Congress, National Referral Center for Science and Technology. Washington, D.C., U.S. Government Printing Office, 1965- . Irregular.

Physical sciences, engineering, 1971. $6.50.
Federal government, 1967. $2.75. (Revised edition scheduled for 1972.)

A series of directories based on the Center's inventory of information resources (see A13). Included are government agencies, research organizations, information centers, and others concerned with fibers, textiles, and dyestuffs.

A4 **DIRECTORY OF SPECIAL LIBRARIES AND INFORMATION CENTERS** Edited by Anthony T. Kruzas. 2nd Edition. Detroit, Gale Research, 1968. 2 Vols. Vol. 1—Special Libraries and Information Centers in the United States and Canada, $28.50; Vol. 2—Geographic-Personnel Index, $23.50.

Volume 1 provides information on the subject specialty, size of collection, staff, and services of special libraries, arranged in alphabetical order by name of library. Eighteen appendices list various U.S. Government special libraries, information centers, and information network systems. The subject index lists approximately 85 special libraries and information centers under the headings: Cotton; Dyes and Pigments; Fibers, synthetic; Textile Chemistry; Textiles; and Wool. Volume 2 is arranged in two sections: one lists alphabetically all library personnel mentioned in Volume 1 with their titles and affiliations; the second lists the libraries by the state and city in which they are located.

A5   **ENCYCLOPEDIA OF ASSOCIATIONS** Edited by Margaret Fisk. 7th Edition. Detroit, Gale Research, 1972. Vol. 1—National Organizations of the United States, $38.50.

Gives address, officers, membership, activities, meeting dates, publications, and other data for more than 16,000 trade associations, professional societies, and other groups, arranged by subject fields. Alphabetical index to organization names and keywords has many textile organizations listed under the entries Dyes, Dyers, Fibers, and Textiles.

A6   **A GUIDE TO SOURCES OF INFORMATION IN THE TEXTILE INDUSTRY** Compiled by members of the Aslib Textile Group. London and Manchester, Aslib and the Textile Institute, 1970. $6.

A comprehensive listing of textile organizations, primary and secondary publications, and sources of various types of documents and information. National and international textile organizations, trade associations, professional societies, and research institutes are included. The listing of textile periodicals is arranged by subject, country of origin, and title. Included in the section on abstract and review publications are current publications in textile and related fields as well as important abstract periodicals no longer being published. Books are arranged in subject order, with publishers and prices for most of them. An extensive list of directories from throughout the world is given. National and international organizations which issue standards applying to textiles are detailed. Patent services and systems of classification are discussed, and sources of patent specifications, including United Kingdom public libraries, are listed. Sources of statistics in periodicals and statistics publications are given. There is no index, but a detailed table of contents is provided.

A7   **A GUIDE FOR THE USE OF THE TEXTILE INFORMATION SYSTEM** By Joanne Butterworth. Masters thesis. Athens, Ga., School of Information Science, Georgia Institute of Technology, 1964.

A detailed review of primary, secondary, and tertiary publications relating to textiles and allied subjects. Publications include those of professional societies, trade associations, government agencies, industrial organizations, textile schools, and commercial publishers. Includes descriptions of publishing records and contents of 100 primary and secondary journals. Contains 381 references and a highly detailed table of contents.

A8 **INDUSTRIAL RESEARCH LABORATORIES OF THE UNITED STATES** Edited by Jacques Cattell Press. 13th Edition. New York, R. R. Bowker, 1970. $39.50.

This edition provides information concerning more than 5,200 nongovernmental research laboratories operated by more than 3,000 organizations. Address, laboratory director, composition of staff, and areas of research are given for each laboratory. Contains personnel, geographic, and subject indexes. Laboratories active in fields related to textiles are listed under subjects such as Bleaching and Bleaching Agents, Cellulose and Cellulose Products, Detergents, Dyes and Dyeing, Extrusion Technology, Fibers, Finishes, Laundry Technology, Pigments, Polymers, Printing, Pulp, Pulping, Surfactants, Textiles, Titanium Pigments, Wool, and Yarns.

A9 **JOURNAL PUBLICATIONS OF INTEREST TO THE TEXTILE INDUSTRY** By P. Jacobs and S. Backer. Cambridge, Mass., Fibers and Polymers Division, Mechanical Engineering Department, Massachusetts Institute of Technology, 1967. Out of print.

A listing of approximately 1,000 unique primary and secondary journal titles and 200 cross-references from former titles to current titles. The journals relate to the textile industry and such associated fields as agriculture, chemistry, physics, mechanical engineering, and others. Each entry contains the publisher or printer, frequency of publication, language(s) of articles published, abstract publications which cover the journal, and libraries known to include the journal among their holdings.

A10 **LIST OF CURRENT PERIODICALS FOR THE TEXTILE AND CLOTHING TRADE** By H. J. Zingel. *Textil-Industrie, 69*:272-281, 484-487, 559-563, 1967. In German.

Part 1 is an alphabetical listing of 725 journals with title, publisher, first year of publication, and language for each entry. Parts 2 and 3 are classifications of these journals by country of publication and subject.

A11 **LITERATURE OF CHEMICAL TECHNOLOGY (No. 78 in Advances in Chemistry Series)** Robert F. Gould, Series Editor. Washington, D.C., American Chemical Society, 1968. $17.50.

Comprised of presentations made at two 1963 symposia sponsored by the Division of Chemical Literature of the American Chemical Society. Most of the presentations were updated to 1968 before publication. Several chapters—with extensive bibliographies—concern textiles or allied subjects: The Literature of Soaps and Detergents; The Literature of Synthetic Dyes; The Literature of Textile Chemistry; The Literature of Textile Utilization and Evaluation; The Literature of Cellulose, Pulp, and Paper; and The Literature of Resins and Plastics. Subject index.

A12 **LITERATURE RESOURCES FOR CHEMICAL PROCESS INDUSTRIES (No. 10 in Advances in Chemistry Series)** Edited by the staff of *Industrial and Engineering Chemistry.* Washington, D.C., American Chemical Society, 1954. $12.

A collection of papers presented at various symposia and general sessions of the Division of Chemical Literature of the American Chemical Society. Chapters which deal specifically with textile information sources are: Editing, Publishing, and Abstracting of Textile Literature; Literature of the Natural Fibers; Literature of Man-Made Fibers; Literature of Dyes, Mordants, and Bleaches; and Literature of Processing and Textile Chemicals. Each chapter has a bibliography. Author and subject indexes.

A13 **NATIONAL REFERRAL CENTER FOR SCIENCE AND TECHNOLOGY** Library of Congress, Washington, D.C. 20540.

The Center functions as an intermediary to direct those requiring information on a particular subject to organizations or individuals with specialized knowledge of that subject. Maintains an inventory of professional societies, university research groups, research institutes, government agencies, industrial laboratories, and individuals, as well as technical libraries, information centers, and abstracting and indexing services. Inventory of information resources contains approximately 125 sources dealing with textile information. Queries to the Center should include a precise statement of the information desired, resources already consulted, and the requester's special qualifications (such as participation in a government contract or membership in a professional society). Requests may be made in person, by telephone, or by letter. Services of the Center are free. Correspondence should be addressed to the Library of Congress, Science and Technology Division, National Referral Center, 10 First St., S.E., Washington, D.C. 20540. Telephone inquiries should be directed to (202) 426-5687 for general information or to 426-5670 for referral service.

A14 **SCIENTIFIC MEETINGS** New York, Special Libraries Association, 1957- . Triannually in January, May, and September. $15/year.

Listings are alphabetical, chronological, and geographical. Subject index includes listings under Fiber and Textiles.

A15 **SUBJECT GUIDE TO BOOKS IN PRINT** New York, R. R. Bowker, 1957- . 2 Vols. Annual. $19.25.

Lists most books published in English and currently in print, giving author, title, publisher, price, and year of publication. Many subject headings apply to the field of textiles and include Clothing Trade; Cotton; Dyes and Dyeing; Fibers; Hemp; Jute; Linen; Rayon; Silk; Textile Chemistry; Textile Design; Textile Fibers; Textile Fibers, Synthetic; Textile Finishing; Textile Industry and Fabrics; Textile Machinery; Textile Printing; and Wool.

A16 **TEXTILE BOOK SERVICE CHECKLIST OF BOOKS IN PRINT**
Metuchen, N.J., Textile Book Service. Free.

Lists approximately 200 current textile and related titles with prices.

A17 **TEXTILE INDUSTRY INFORMATION SOURCES Annotated Guide to the Literature of Textile Fibers, Dyes and Dyeing, Design and Decoration, Weaving, Machinery, and other subjects.** By Joseph V. Kopycinski. Detroit, Gale Research, 1964. Management Information Guide No. 4. $8.75.

The first section provides an annotated list of reference materials including encyclopedias, handbooks, dictionaries, abstract and review publications, bibliographies, and directories. The second and largest section lists books—many of historical interest—by subject category. The final section covers educational, industrial, government, and public libraries with good textile collections. Subject and author indexes.

A18 **THE TEXTILE LIBRARY   A Selected List of Books**   Compiled by Mary E. Bragg. Charlottesville, Va., Institute of Textile Technology, 1966. 1966-1969 Supplement. Free. From: Roger Milliken Textile Library, Institute of Textile Technology, Charlottesville, Va. 22902.

Compiled primarily to provide the Institute's member mills with a useful list of books relating to the various areas of textile technology. Basic publication lists 257 books, pamphlets, and other material. Supplement contains listings for 154 additional books. Both are arranged by subject and contain author indexes.

A19 **ULRICH'S INTERNATIONAL PERIODICALS DIRECTORY**   New York, R. R. Bowker, 1932- . 2 Vols. Biennial. $34.50/set.

The 13th edition (1969-1970) provides information for more than 40,000 periodical titles including first year of publication, publisher, frequency of publication, cost, and a brief description of subject matter. Textile and related publications are listed under such headings as Cleaning and Dyeing, Clothing Trade, Textile Industries, and Fabrics. Subject and title indexes.

A20 **WORLD MEETINGS: OUTSIDE UNITED STATES AND CANADA**
New York, World Meetings Information Center, 1968- . Quarterly. $35/year. From: WMIC, CCM Information Corporation, 866 Third Ave., New York, N.Y. 10022.

The format and contents of this publication are similar to those of *World Meetings: United States and Canada* (see A21).

A21 **WORLD MEETINGS: UNITED STATES AND CANADA** New York, World Meetings Information Center, 1967- . Quarterly. $35/year. From: WMIC, CCM Information Corporation, 866 Third Ave., New York, N.Y. 10022.

Meetings are listed by date, keywords, deadline for paper or abstract, location, and sponsor. Meetings relating to textiles appear under the keywords Fiber and Textile.

2

Information on Ongoing Research and Development

To avoid duplication of research or development work which may be underway in another laboratory and to take full advantage of related work, it is necessary that R&D directors and scientists use all relevant sources of ongoing research available. The proprietary nature of much industrial R&D work precludes obtaining data about many current projects. However, information concerning some ongoing industrial research projects and many research institute and government-sponsored projects is available through a number of sources.

The means of obtaining information about active research and development projects on which no final reports have been published are described in this chapter.

Part B: Polymer Letters of the *Journal of Polymer Science* publishes short accounts of very recent research results—some of which apply to fibers and textiles. No similar publication dealing specifically with current textile R&D work is available at present. However, this kind of information may be found in the notes, letters, or communications sections of other polymer journals and some textile journals.

Other sources of information about ongoing research relevant to fibers and textiles are: government publications which include progress reports of government-sponsored R&D; annual reports of research organizations, trade associations, colleges, and universities in which topics of current research are listed; and the Science Information Exchange, which provides summaries of research in progress in industrial organizations, research institutes, trade associations, and government departments.

B1   **CURRENT RESEARCH INFORMATION SYSTEM (CRIS)**   U.S. Department of Agriculture, Washington, D.C. 20250.

A service which provides information about current research funded by USDA agencies, state agricultural experimental stations, and other cooperating institutions. Included is information on R&D work related to cotton, wool, and selection and care of clothing and household textiles. This service is available only to Department of Agriculture researchers, but CRIS accounts of research in progress are provided to the Science Information Exchange (see B13).

B2   **FIBRE SCIENCE AND TECHNOLOGY**   London, Elsevier Publishing Co. Ltd., 1968- . Quarterly. Approximately $25/year.

"Technical Notes" contained therein frequently cover current research results. Also contains full accounts of completed research studies.

B3   **GOVERNMENT REPORTS ANNOUNCEMENTS (GRA)**   (Formerly *U.S. Government Research and Development Reports*) Springfield, Va., National Technical Information Service (formerly Clearinghouse for Federal Scientific and Technical Information), 1946- . Semimonthly. $30/year.

Announcement bulletin for reports of research and development work performed under government contracts, including progress reports. Abstracts are classified under COSATI subject headings and include Fibers and Textiles under Materials. Indexes are available in a separate publication, *Government Reports Index* (see D15).

B4   **JOURNAL OF APPLIED POLYMER SCIENCE**   New York, Interscience Publishers, 1959- . Monthly. $150/year, including *Applied Polymer Symposia.*
"Notes" section may provide information developed in current research work.

B5   **JOURNAL OF COLLOID AND INTERFACE SCIENCE**   New York, Academic Press, 1966- . Four volumes/year. Monthly. $32/volume.
Contains "Notes" and "Letters to the Editor" which include information relating to ongoing research and development projects.

B6   **JOURNAL OF MATERIALS SCIENCE**   London, Chapman and Hall, 1966- . Monthly. $62.40/year.
Letters in this *Journal* contain comments based on recent research not yet published. Also contains full reports of research work.

B7   **JOURNAL OF POLYMER SCIENCE, PART B: POLYMER LETTERS** New York, Interscience Publishers, 1963- . Monthly. $325/year, including *Part A-1: Polymer Chemistry; Part A-2: Polymer Physics;* and *Part C: Polymer Symposia.*
Polymer Letters prints only those items considered novel and current enough to deserve publication in abbreviated and preliminary form. Those which do not meet these criteria may be published in other parts of the *Journal of Polymer Science.*

B8   **JOURNAL OF THE SOCIETY OF DYERS AND COLOURISTS** Bradford, England, Society of Dyers and Colourists, 1884- . Monthly. Approximately $30/year.
Correspondence section offers comments by *Journal* readers, often accompanied by recent research data. Contains detailed reports of completed research, activities of the society, and book reviews.

B9   **JOURNAL OF THE TEXTILE INSTITUTE**   Manchester, England,

Textile Institute, 1910- . Monthly. Approximately $62/year, including *Textile Institute and Industry* and *Textile Progress.* "Letters to the Editor" frequently includes results of ongoing research. Also includes detailed articles reporting the results of completed research projects.

B10 **MACROMOLECULES** Washington, D.C., American Chemical Society, 1968- . Bimonthly. $12/year to members; $24/year to nonmembers.

Contains "Notes" and "Communications to the Editor" which give results obtained in current projects. Also includes full reports of research projects already completed.

B11 **NATURE (London)** London, Macmillan Journals Ltd., 1869- . Weekly. $48/year.

Letters published under "Physical Sciences" sometimes provide current information on research related to fibers, particularly carbon and graphite fibers.

B12 **POLYMER** Guildford, England, Iliffe Science and Technology Publications Ltd., 1960- . Monthly. $56/year in U.S.; $84/year for air mail.

"Notes and Communications" section provides comments of workers in fields of research related to fibers in which recent results are reported. Contains formal reports of completed research work as well.

B13 **SCIENCE INFORMATION EXCHANGE (SIE)** 300 Madison National Bank Bldg., 1730 M St., N.W., Washington, D.C. 20036.

SIE maintains computer files of research projects in progress or recently completed. Research summaries are obtained from the organization supporting the work or directly from the principal investigator, not from progress reports or journal articles. Consequently, SIE provides information which is not, and may not be, available in the published literature.

The Exchange stores and retrieves several hundred ongoing research summaries each year concerning textiles and related technology. Research work described is supported by organizations such as the U.S. Department of Agriculture, Textile Research Institute, American Carpet Institute, Cotton Research Committee of Texas, U.S. Department of Defense, and others.

Subject searches are performed with an IBM 360/40 computer for $50 per question ($30 for each additional question submitted on the same purchase order). Quarterly mailings of subject information are provided for fees of $60 for the initial mailing and $35 for each automatic quarterly mailing. These fees cover the first 100 documents retrieved (average number of documents retrieved per search is 60). A fee of $10 is charged for each additional 100 documents or fraction thereof.

Requests for services may be made by telephone or mail. Mail should be addressed to Science Information Exchange, Room 300, 1730 M Street, N.W., Washington, D.C. 20036. Telephone requests should be made to (202) 381-5511 for information in the Physical Sciences or 381-5721 for information in the Life Sciences.

B14 **SCIENTIFIC RESEARCH IN BRITISH UNIVERSITIES AND COLLEGES** London, Great Britain Department of Education and Science and the British Council, 1950- . Annual. Price varies. From: British Information Services, 845 Third Ave., New York, N.Y. 10022.

Includes research in the field of textile technology and gives titles of research projects and names of supervisory personnel for each.

B15 **SCIENTIFIC AND TECHNICAL AEROSPACE REPORTS (STAR)** National Aeronautics and Space Administration. Washington, D.C., U.S. Government Printing Office, 1963- . Semimonthly. $54/year.

Abstract journal covering the world's report literature on the science and technology of aeronautics. Progress reports are included. Abstracts are arranged in classified order. Information on textiles appears under Materials, Non-Metallic.

Subject, personal author, corporate source, report/accession number, and accession/report number indexes in each issue.

B16   **TECHNICAL ABSTRACT BULLETIN (TAB)**   Alexandria, Va., Defense Documentation Center, 1953- . Semimonthly. Free to qualified DDC users.

Contains abstracts of classified and limited distribution reports of research and development work performed under the sponsorship of the Department of Defense and available at the Defense Documentation Center. Abstracts of reports, including progress reports, are arranged in classified order. Reports relating to textiles are abstracted under Fibers and Textiles, a subheading under Materials. Indexes are published separately (see D40).

B17   **TEXTILE RESEARCH JOURNAL**   Princeton, N.J., Textile Research Institute, 1930- . $50/year.

Results of current research projects often are reported in "Short Communications and Letters" section. Also contains detailed reports of completed research work and book reviews.

Information on recent and current research also is published in the annual reports of many research institutes and industry associations. In general, these reports are available to anyone requesting them. A few representative organizations publishing such material are:

B18   **COMMONWEALTH SCIENTIFIC AND INDUSTRIAL RESEARCH ORGANIZATION (CSIRO)**   Wool Research Laboratories, 343 Royal Parade, Parkville, Melbourne, Australia.

Publishes detailed accounts of recent and continuing research work of the Divisions of Protein Chemistry, Textile Physics, and Textile Industry. Also includes lists of published papers and patents granted.

B19   **COTTON PRODUCERS INSTITUTE**   P.O. Box 12253, Memphis, Tenn. 38112.

Research projects to be performed in the coming year by

universities and research institutes under the sponsorship of
the Cotton Producers Institute are described in *Cotton Research Notes*. Research includes agricultural studies, quality
evaluation, chemical finishing, and end-use applications. Brief
reports of recent research are also included.

B20   **DANSK TEXTIL INSTITUT**   Stokhusgade 5, Copenhagen, Denmark.
Annual review of the research activities of the Institute are
published in *Tidsskrift for Textileknik*. In Danish.

B21   **INDIAN CENTRAL JUTE COMMITTEE**   12 Regent Park, Calcutta-40, India.
Current research of the Technological Researches Laboratories related to jute, sisal, and other bast fibers is reviewed in
the annual report.

B22   **INSTITUT TEXTILE DE FRANCE (ITF)**   35 rue des Abondances,
Boulogne-sur-Seine, France.
Offers reviews of results of recent research by the Institute
and seven affiliated research laboratories. Gives brief preview
of research work for the coming year and a list of studies
previously reported in *Bulletin de l'Institut Textile de France*.
In French.
Bulletin de l'Institut Textile de France ceased publication
in 1971. The reports formerly appearing in the *Bulletin* are
now published as *Bulletin Scientifique de l'Institut Textile de
France*.

B23   **INTERNATIONAL WOOL SECRETARIAT**   Wool House, 6-7 Carlton Gardens, London, S.W. 1, England.
The annual report, which reviews recent research work and
discusses research in progress, is published in *World Wool
Digest*.

B24   **NATIONAL COTTON COUNCIL OF AMERICA**   Ring Building,
1200 18th St., N.W., Washington, D.C. 20036.

Research activities for the previous and coming years are reviewed in *Cotton's Progress*.

B25 **SOUTH AFRICAN WOOL TEXTILE RESEARCH INSTITUTE (SAWTRI)** P.O. Box 1124, Port Elizabeth, South Africa.
SAWTRI report contains brief descriptions of recent and current research in Protein Chemistry, Scouring, Dyeing, and Finishing; Textile Physics, Statistics, Testing Services, Carding, Combing, and Spinning; Weaving and Knitting; and Fundamental Wool Protein Chemistry.

B26 **SVENSKA TEXTILFORSKNINGSINSTITUTET** Gibraltargatan 5F, Göteberg, Sweden.
Brief accounts of current research projects are given. In Swedish.

B27 **TEXTILE RESEARCH INSTITUTE (TRI)** P.O. Box 625, Princeton, N.J. 08540.
Discusses results of recent research related to natural and manmade fibers and fiber assemblies. Describes the objectives of current member-supported special research programs. Lists subjects of current textile research by predoctoral fellows at Princeton and other universities.

B28 **UNIVERSITY OF MANCHESTER INSTITUTE OF SCIENCE AND TECHNOLOGY (UMIST)** P.O. Box 88, Manchester, M60 1QD, England.
Lists research in progress in the Departments of Polymer and Fibre Science and Textile Technology.

B29 **WOOL INDUSTRIES RESEARCH ASSOCIATION (WIRA)** Torridon, Headingley Lane, Leeds 6, England.
Annual report of the director of research discusses WIRA's current research work.

3

Current Awareness Services

The current awareness services discussed in this chapter rely, in general, on recently published documents that describe results of R&D work which may have been completed several years earlier. For example, many scientific journals require compliance with a standard article format and acceptance by a review board for all papers they publish. This often results in a delay of at least several months between completion of an R&D project and publication of the results. Similarly, the average interval of three to four years between filing of a U.S. patent application and issuance and publication of the patent creates a considerable time lag in the publication of R&D results which may not have appeared elsewhere. Since the journal and patent literature constitutes a large portion of the information covered by current awareness services, and further delay can be introduced by abstracting the documents and printing an abstract bulletin, "current" is a relative term. For the results of truly current R&D work, the sources described in the previous chapter should be used.

In spite of the delays inherent in most current awareness services, they serve a very useful purpose. Because they generally select for coverage only the most significant documents, from publications which also may be available to the researcher, they save him the time of per-

sonally scanning these publications. In addition, most current awareness services include documents—relevant to their subject areas—from
many fringe publications which may be acquired only by very large
R&D facilities.

The most common type of current awareness service in the textile
field is the abstract bulletin. Most of these are arranged by subject
categories to allow the user to scan only those portions which relate
to his specific interests. Many of these publications include author
and subject indexes to each issue. Typical of this kind of service are
the *Alerting Bulletins* of the *Central Patents Index* produced by Derwent Publications Ltd. The *Bulletins* contain abstracts of U.S., European, Japanese, and other patents (see Figure 1) and are available
arranged by subject classification or by country. The *Bulletins* include
patent number, patentee, and other indexes to the patents abstracted
in each weekly issue.

A variation of the abstract bulletin is the primary journal which includes an abstracts section. It is generally of relatively limited scope in
comparison to the secondary publications. In many instances, the
abstracts sections of primary journals are in classified order and have
indexes. A related type of alerting service, which in addition performs
a Selective Dissemination of Information (SDI) function, is provided
by the bulletins distributed by the *Fast Announcement Service* (FAS)
of the National Technical Information Service. These bulletins, available in many subject categories, announce receipt by NTIS of new
government R&D reports.

Two textile information sources also offer SDI services to their subscribers. *Textile Technology Digest* provides copies of abstracts from
the *Digest* which relate to the subject or subjects specified by the subscriber. L'Institut Textile de France will provide magnetic tapes which
are excerpts of those portions of its TITUS tapes that relate to documents in specific subject areas.

CA Condensates—another current awareness service—provides magnetic tapes containing titles, authors, references, and keyterms (single
words or phrases which describe important concepts, e.g., carding,
disperse dyes, or second order transition temperature) for all documents abstracted in *Chemical Abstracts*. These tapes are used by information service centers and private organizations to provide SDI services

27217S   A81-F8-(A11-A28)   +GB 1230379
Application of adhesive to sheet materials.
    Flexible composite sheet comprises a compressed
cellular plastics sheet adhered to a fibrous textile
or cellular plastics material. The bonding agent is
sprayed on to at least one of the component sheets in
a discontinuous pattern.
    The discontinuous pattern is pref. achieved by
using an adhesive of high viscosity which is emitted
from the nozzle in a stringy spray. The adhesive is
a two part polyurethane composition containing 20.25%
solids and having a viscosity of 900-1300 cP.   30.10.68
(clg. 4.11.67; 2.4.68-GB-003739; 015711) B32b-5/18
(28.4.71) DUNLOP CO. LTD.

17870Q   A14-F1-(A94)   =GB 1230392
Acrylonitrile fibre of non-circular cross-section.
    The fibres are formed from a spinning soln. of
polyacrylonitrile or a copolymer of it with at least one
ethylenically unsatd. copolymerisable monomer contg.
>50 wt.% of acrylonitrile units, dissolved in an aqs.
soln. of an inorganic salt or salts, by extruding
through a spinneret formed from an inert non-metallic
material of thermal conductivity $\not> 5 \times 10^{-3}$ cal. cm^{-1}
sec^{-1}. deg^{-1}, into an aqs. coagulating bath whose temp.
is   10°C, the temp of the spinning soln. being at least
30°C higher than this temp. The spinneret is provided
with at least one orifice of non-circular cross-section
which satisfies the relationship $2 \leqslant R_J \leqslant 9$, in which
9, in which R_J = length of long axis: length of short
axis of the orifice cross-section, and the jet drafting
ration S_J on extrusion satisfies the relationship $4 \leqslant$
$R_J.S_J$, where S_J is the "drawing speed" of the coagu-
lated fibre : Aver. linear velocity of spinning soln.
passing through the orifice, where " drawing speed"
is the linear speed at which the fibres are taken up
from the coagulating bath. 25.6.68 as 030328 (clg.
28.6.67-JA-041812) D01f-7/02, 7/06. (28.4.71)
JAPAN EXLAN CO. LTD

FIGURE 1. Typical abstracts from the *Alerting Bulletin* of the *Textiles, Paper* section of *Central Patents Index* for week S16 (1971).

to individual scientists and engineers. The interests of each user of
the service are described by keyterms (see Figure 2) which constitute
his interest profile. This profile is compared by computer with the title
and keyterms of each document entered on the Condensates tapes.
For each document matching the interest profile, full descriptive information is printed (see Figure 3). The computer-produced printout of

```
FRCFILE NC. 6C50-CC5
ACCCUNT NC.                                    THRESHOLD WT.   CCC00

CATA BASE SEARCHED  CA VOLUME 74 ISSUE 16

                               PRCFILE

GRCUP    TERM    TYPE    WEIGHT              TERM
         NC.

GCC1      1      TXT     00CCC      *DYE*
GCC1      2      CAS     00CCC      C4C*

GCC2      3      TXT     001CC      CARRIER*
GCC2      4      TXT     001CC      SWELLING*
GCC2      5      TXT     001CC      ASSIST*
GCC2      6      TXT     001CC      LEVEL*
GCO2      7      TXT     001CC      AUXILIAR*
GCC2      8      TXT     00CCC      PCLYESTER*
GCC2      9      TXT     00CCC      PCLYLESTER*
GCC2     1C      TXT     00CCC      *ETHYLENE TEREPHTHALATE*
GOO2     11      TXT     00CCC      *ETHYLENE GLYCOL TEREPHTHALATE*
GCC2     12      TXT     00CCC      *ETHYLENE PHTHALATE*
GCO2     13      TXT     00CCC      *CYCLOHEXYLENEDIMETHYLENE TEREPHT
                                     HALATE*
GOO2     14      TXT     00CCC      CACRON
GCC2     15      TXT     00CCC      KCCEL
GCC2     16      TXT     00CCC      LAVSAN
GCC2     17      TXT     00CCC      TERYLENE

GCC1*GCO2

NUMBER OF ANSWERS TO THIS QUESTION  17
```

FIGURE 2. Input for current awareness search of CA Condensates magnetic tape covering Volume 74, Issue 16 of *Chemical Abstracts*. The individual's interests in carrier dyeing and dyeing of polyester fibers are converted into his interest profile, which consists of combinations of search terms.

all matches is the SDI product provided to the user.

Machine-readable files provided by other information services also can be used to generate listings of documents relevant to the specific interests of individual users. These are the Chemical Abstracts Service's POST tapes, which contain full reference information and abstracts in which keywords are identified; l'Institut Textile de France's TITUS magnetic tapes, which store bibliographic citations, abstracts, and key-terms for each document; *World Textile Abstracts'* magnetic tapes, which include full reference information, keyterms, and characterization codes for the type of document and its contents; and *Textile Technology Digest's* punched cards or magnetic tapes, which contain keyterms and abstract numbers in sequential order.

Chemical Titles, which is a computer-produced permuted index or KWIC (keyword-in-context) index (see Figure 4), is a different form of current awareness publication. As a result of permutation, each document title appears in the alphabetical index under each significant term

```
**************************************************************
  PRCFILE NC. 6C50-CC5              FRIDAY, APRIL 23, 1971
                                         QUESTION NT. 20C

  ANTAKI AS,
  NATL. RES. CENT., COKKI, UAR

     CARRIER-ASSISTED CYEINC

  KCLCR. ERT.(KCERAS) 1970, 12(11-12) 277-8C

  REVIEW SCLVENTS DYEINC TEXTILES

  CA-CCNCENSATES(CHAEA8) 1971, C74(16) C7726?

  **************************************************************

  PRCFILE NC. 6C50-CC5              FRIDAY, APRIL 23, 1971
                                         QUESTION NT. 1CC

  SCHMICT F,CRCZC I,
  INST. WLCKIEN SZTLC. SYNTET., POL.

     PCSSIEILITY OF A LEVEL CYEINC CF WOVEN AND KNIITEC STYLCN FAB
     RICS WITH PCL I9H ACID CYES

  PRZEGL. WLCK.(PRZWAZ) 197C, 24(8-5) 4(7-9

  ACIC CYES PCLYAMICE FABRICS STYLCN CYEING POLISH

  CA-CCNCENSATES(CHAEA8) 1971, C74(16) C7725E

  **************************************************************
```

FIGURE 3. A portion of the output from the current awareness search of CA Condensates described in Figure 2. For each retrieved document, the bibliographic citation, keywords, and *Chemical Abstracts* reference are given.

in the title. Each title is identified by a code which can be converted to the document source in another section of the publication. *Chemical Titles* also is available on magnetic tape for machine searching, usually for SDI purposes. While KWIC indexes—which require no human analysis of document content—are relatively fast and inexpensive to produce, their usefulness is limited by the titles' inherent accuracy and completeness regarding the subject matter of the documents.

Publications containing abstracts of papers to be presented at professional society meetings provide information about recent R&D work in advance of formal publication. Typical examples are: *Polymer Preprints,* which abstracts papers to be delivered before the Polymer Division of the American Chemical Society and is issued before each semiannual national meeting of the Society, and *Textile Chemist and Colorist,* which publishes abstracts of papers to be presented at the annual AATCC meeting. A similar opportunity is afforded through announcements by some of the primary journals of prepublication avail-

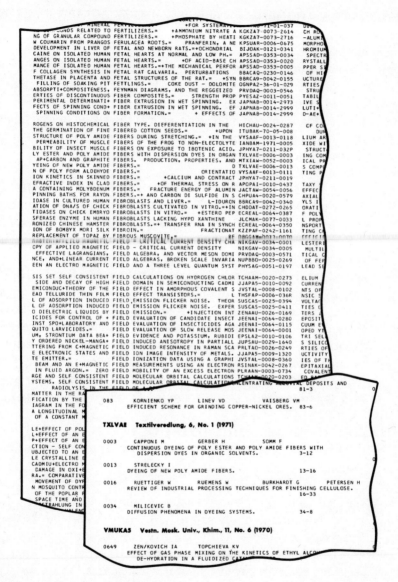

FIGURE 4. Excerpt from *Chemical Titles* for February 22, 1971, showing titles containing the words FIBER and FIBERS in the permuted (KWIC) index. Entry for "DYFING OF NEW POLYAMIDE FIBERS" has reference code TXLVAL-0006-0013 which leads to the journal citation for that article in the Bibliography.

ability of papers scheduled for print. Some issues of *TAPPI* list papers being considered for publication and give instructions for obtaining them immediately.

Finally, although it is certainly not the traditional type of current awareness service, the *Daily News Record* cannot be overlooked as a source of very current fiber and textile information. While the emphasis of this publication is on commercial aspects of the textile industry, new technical developments are well covered and generally much earlier than in other textile publications.

C1   **ABSTRACT BULLETIN OF THE INSTITUTE OF PAPER CHEMISTRY**
Appleton, Wis., Institute of Paper Chemistry, 1930- . Monthly. $75/year to nonmembers; $25/year to academic institutions.

Documents abstracted are selected from most of the 700 periodicals (including about 100 abstract publications) received by the Institute's library. Abstracts of articles, books, and dissertations are published in a classified arrangement which includes the headings: Cellulose and Cellulose Derivatives, Cellulosic Textiles, Fibers, Pulp, Pulp Manufacture, Pulp Treatment, and Pulpwood and Other Fibrous Raw Materials. Patents from the United States, Great Britain, USSR, Germany, France, Canada, and other countries are abstracted in a separate section and arranged by subject classification.

C2   **BULLETIN DE L'INSTITUT TEXTILE DE FRANCE***   Paris, l'Institut Textile de France, 1948--. Bimonthly. Approximately $25/year for U.S. subscribers. In French.

Each issue provides abstracts of articles and French patents selected from about 400 periodicals published throughout the world (including many from Latin American and Eastern European countries). Titles are given in the original language and in French. Journal and patent abstracts are in separate sections, each arranged by subject categories. Major subject classifications are: Fibers; Transformation of Fibers into Yarns; Transformation of the Structure of Yarns (includes twisting, plying, texturing); Transformation of Yarns or Fibers into Fabrics (knit, woven, nonwoven); Finishing (includes bleaching, dyeing, printing); Transformation of Textile Structures into Finished Articles; Maintenance of Textiles (laundering, drycleaning, etc.); Analysis, Testing, and Control; Study of Polymers; Industrial Organization; Industrial Management; Documentation; and Teaching-Research.

Abstracts published in the *Bulletin,* including keyterms, constitute a large part of the information stored on the TITUS magnetic tapes (see D10). These tapes are in appropriate format for use in Selective Dissemination of Information (SDI) programs.

Bulletin de l'Institut Textile de France ceased publication at the end of 1971. The reports formerly published in the *Bulletin* now appear in *Bulletin Scientifique de l'Institut Textile de France.* The abstracts which had been published in the *Bulletin* are now being published in *l'Industrie Textile* (Paris, Editions de l'Industrie Textile, 1884- , monthly, approximately $24/year). These abstracts and keyterms selected for the documents are still used as input to the Institut's TITUS system.

C3　**CA CONDENSATES** Columbus, Ohio, Chemical Abstracts Service of the American Chemical Society, 1968- . Weekly. $4,400/year including one printed copy of *Chemical Abstracts.*

Magnetic tape service for all abstracts published in *Chemical Abstracts* (see D12). Available in the new Standard Distribution Format only. Tapes contain title, author, full reference information, and keyword index entries for each document. To retrieve information from the tapes, subjects, keyword roots, authors, compound names, or journal CODEN can be used with either Boolean logic or weighted-term strategies (see Figure 2). Output provides full bibliographic citation, *CA* abstract number, and keyword entries (see Figure 3).

Entries for documents abstracted in *CA* are stored on magnetic tapes in serial or sequential (abstract number) order so that the full tape must be scanned to retrieve information relevant to, for example, a single compound. Consequently, because of this problem and the large number of documents abstracted each week, computer processing times are lengthy. As a result, CA Condensates is more suitable for current awareness use, in which a large number of interest profiles can be compared with the tapes in a single search each week, than for retrospective searching which might require scanning tapes for many weeks for only a few questions. A number of information centers do, however, offer current awareness or retrospective searching services for CA Condensates (see E7, E15, E20, and E21).

C4   **CENTRAL PATENTS INDEX (CPI)**   London, Derwent Publications Ltd., 1970- . Weekly.

Patent documentation service in several sections. Covers patents from 12 major industrial countries including the United States, Great Britain, USSR, Belgium, France, Germany, and the Netherlands. Weekly *Alerting Bulletins* contain abstracts which include specification number, publication date, patentee, filing and priority dates, *CPI* classification, and *International Patent Classification*, as well as a brief description of the invention (see Figure 1). The *Alerting Bulletin* is available in either country or classified order. *Alerting Bulletins* contain patent-number, *CPI*-class, patentee, and equivalent-to-basic indexes for the patents covered in each issue.

———— **CHEMDOC**   London, Derwent Publications Ltd., 1970- . Weekly. Partial basic subscription $1,250/year, plus $32/year for *Alerting Bulletin* in country order or $30/year for *Alerting Bulletin* in classified order.

Dyestuffs, one of three subdivisions of *CHEMDOC*, covers azo, anthraquinone, heterocyclic, and other dyes and precursors.

———— **PLASDOC**   London, Derwent Publications Ltd., 1966- . Weekly. Partial basic subscription $1,250/year, plus $54/year for *Alerting Bulletin* in country order or $51/year for *Alerting Bulletin* in classified order.

Classifications are: Additions and Natural Polymers; Condensation Polymers; Processing; General Additives and Applications; Monomers and Condensants; Polymerization Controllers; Additives and Compounding Agents; Polymer Manufacture; and Applications. Fiber-forming polymers are covered under the first two classifications and the production of fibers is included under the Processing heading. Dyes and pigments are included under Additives and Compounding Agents. Categories included under Applications are: Clothing, footwear; Textile auxiliaries; and Semifinished materials—fibres, films, foams.

———— **TEXTILES; PAPER** London, Derwent Publications Ltd., 1970- . Weekly. Partial basic subscription $625/year, plus $22/year for *Alerting Bulletin* in country order or $20/year for *Alerting Bulletin* in classified order.

Patent abstracts are arranged under these headings: Threads and fibres—natural or artificial, spinning; Yarns, mechanical finishing of yarns or ropes, warping or beaming; Weaving; Braiding, knitting—including trimmings and non-woven fabrics; Sewing, embroidering, tufting; Chemical type treatment of textiles; Other textile treatment; Flexible sheet materials—consisting of polymer-coated fibrous web; and Paper-making, production of cellulose. Approximately 500 patents abstracted in each issue.

C5 **CHEMICAL TITLES** Columbus, Ohio, Chemical Abstracts Service of the American Chemical Society, 1960- . Biweekly. $60/year; $30/year to ACS members; discounts on purchases of 50 or more copies.

A keyword-in-context (KWIC) index of titles of selected papers from about 700 of the world's chemical journals including approximately 10 journals related to textile and dye-stuff chemistry and 20 or more polymer science journals. Each issue contains about 5,000 titles and consists of three sections: "Keyword-in-Context Index," "Bibliography," and "Author Index." Each title in the two Indexes is identified by a reference code which leads to the Bibliography section in which full citations are given (see Figure 4). Entries in the Bibliography are arranged by journal title so that this section serves as a table of contents for each of the journal issues covered. No volume indexes.

Also offered on magnetic tape for $1,700 per year including one copy of the printed index. Available beginning with 1962 issues. Three information centers offering searching services for *Chemical Titles* magnetic tapes are listed in E15, E20, and E21.

C6   **DAILY NEWS RECORD**   New York, Fairchild Publications, 1892- . Daily, Monday through Friday. $24/year.

This very popular newspaper provides the means of following financial, commercial, and technical developments in the world of textiles and fashion. Includes announcements of new fibers, new fiber types, and fiber price changes; new developments in textile processes and machinery; financial statements of corporations with operations relating to fibers and textiles; production, consumption, and market forecasts for fibers, yarns, and fabrics; legislation affecting the textile industry; and retailing and fashion.

C7   **FAST ANNOUNCEMENT SERVICE (FAS)**   Springfield, Va., National Technical Information Service (formerly Clearinghouse for Federal Scientific and Technical Information). Irregular. $5/year.

Announcement bulletins for selected new government R&D reports received by NTIS. Any or all of the 57 subject categories may be received through a single subscription. Frequency of publication is determined by receipt of reports. Category 18, Fibers and Textiles, covers natural and manmade fibers, yarns, fabrics, and clothing. Other categories of possible interest are Chemical Processing (7); Cleaning and Finishing (9); Composite Mixed Materials (12); Control Systems and Instrumentation (13); Optics (32); Plastics (35); Quality Control, Standards, Specifications (38); Sanitation and Pollution (41); Testing, Analysis (44); Wood and Paper (46); and Materials Deterioration (57).

C8   **HOSIERY ABSTRACTS**   Nottingham, England, Hosiery and Allied Trades Research Association (HATRA), 1949- . Bimonthly. Approximately $18/year.

Approximately 150 textile journals, standards and trade publications, U.S. and British Patent Office listings, and a few abstract bulletins are scanned for documents related to production of hosiery and other knit products. Abstracts are arranged under 13 classifications: Fibres; Yarn Production; Winding and Warping; Fabric Production; Hosiery Production; Making-Up; Dyeing and Printing; Chemical and Finishing Processes; Laundering and Dry-Cleaning; Analysis, Testing, Grading, and Defects; Sciences; Management; and Generalities. Approximately 1,300 abstracts were published in 1970. Those of lasting interest also are published in *World Textile Abstracts* (see C24) and are included in its indexes.

C9 **JOURNAL OF APPLIED CHEMISTRY AND BIOTECHNOLOGY (Abstracts Section)** (Formerly *Journal of Applied Chemistry*) London, Society of Chemical Industry, 1951- . Monthly. $48/year.

Contains abstracts of British patents and articles selected from worldwide journals. Each issue includes several hundred abstracts of which approximately one-fourth cover patents. Abstracts of articles, followed by patent abstracts, are arranged in a single subject classification. Subjects which relate to fiber-forming polymers, fibers, textile processing, and dyestuffs are: Safety and Hygiene (covers flammability of textiles); Industrial Organic Chemistry (includes dyestuffs); Detergents; Paper (includes Cellulose and Wood Products, Pulp and Paper); and Fibres, Polymers, Paints (covers fibers, fiber production, textiles, and textile processing). Author index, which includes corporate authors, and subject index to numbered abstracts published in each issue.

C10 **JOURNAL OF THE SOCIETY OF DYERS AND COLOURISTS (Abstracts Section)** Bradford, England, The Society of Dyers and Colourists, 1884- . Monthly. Approximately $30/year.

Monthly issues contain about 300 abstracts of articles and U.S. and British patents selected from about 100 sources. Journal abstracts, followed by patent abstracts, are arranged in a single subject classification. Subject headings are: Plant, Machinery, Buildings; Water and Effluents; Chemicals, Auxiliary Products, Finishing Materials; Raw Materials, Intermediates, Colouring Matters; Paints, Enamels, Inks; Fibres, Yarns, Fabrics; Desizing, Scouring, Carbonising, Bleaching; Dyeing; Printing; Finishing; Paper and Other Cellulosic Products; Leather, Furs, Other Protein Materials; Rubber, Resins, Plastics; Analysis, Testing, Apparatus; Colour Physics and Measurement; Automation and Instrumentation; and Miscellaneous.

C11 **OFFICIAL GAZETTE OF THE UNITED STATES PATENT OFFICE** U.S. Patent Office. Washington, D.C., U.S. Government Printing Office, 1872- . Weekly. $78/year.

Includes decisions in patent cases, patent suits, reissues, and defensive publications. Main body of the *Gazette* provides abstracts (or major claims) of patents granted in the week covered. Design patents and trademarks also included. Patents are classified by type: General and Mechanical, Chemical, or Electrical. Most textile processing and extrusion equipment patents are found in the General and Mechanical section; most patents covering fiber-forming polymers, polymerization, extrusion processes, dyestuffs, finishing agents, and dyeing and finishing are contained in the Chemical section.

C12 **PLASTICS INDUSTRY NOTES** Columbus, Ohio, Chemical Abstracts Service of the American Chemical Society, 1967- . Weekly. $225/year.

An abstract publication for marketing, management, and production personnel. Information on polymers and plastics is abstracted from 30 trade journals and newspapers. Abstracts are arranged in 11 sections: Production/Consumption, Prices, Marketing/Sales, Plant Expansion, New Products/ Uses, Corporate Transactions, Government Action, Licensing/ Patent Actions, State-of-the-Art Surveys, Management Changes, and Safety.

Each issue contains about 450 abstracts in which keywords

are capitalized. Names of companies, individuals, products, and other subjects are indexed. Keyword index in each issue.

C13 **POLYMER PREPRINTS** New York, Division of Polymer Chemistry, American Chemical Society, 1960- . Semiannual. $12/year.

Contains in-depth abstracts of papers to be presented before the Division of Polymer Chemistry at semiannual national meetings of the American Chemical Society. Published in advance of the meeting covered. Includes papers which might be published at a much later date. Author index.

C14 **POLYMER SCIENCE & TECHNOLOGY (POST)** Columbus, Ohio, Chemical Abstracts Service of the American Chemical Society, 1967- . Biweekly. $2,500/year.

Available only as a computer-readable file, POST provides abstracts of the world's journal and report literature and patents from 26 countries. Subject coverage related to textiles includes the synthesis and properties of monomers and polymers for fibers; chemical and physical properties of natural organic and manmade fibers; and the manufacture (extrusion, drawing), chemical treatment (stabilization, dyeing, finishing), and uses of fibers, including apparatus for fiber preparation and treatment. A *Keyword Subject Index* is provided. Two information centers (see E7 and E20) offer current awareness services for the POST tapes.

C15 **PUBLICATIONS AND PATENTS** Agricultural Research Service, Southern Marketing and Nutrition Research Division. New Orleans, U.S. Department of Agriculture. Semiannual. Free.

An annotated bibliography of published papers and patents of personnel of the Division. Included are those related to chemical modification, finishing, processing, and structure of cotton. Subject index in each issue.

C16 **RAPRA ABSTRACTS** Shawbury, England, Rubber and Plastics

Research Association of Great Britain, 1965- . Weekly. $160/year.

Covers material from approximately 300 journals; U.S., British, and French patents; conference reports; and additions to the RAPRA library printed in separate sections and arranged by subject classification. Includes abstracts of documents on polymers used in the manufacture of fibers, extrusion of fibers, fibers as fillers for plastics and rubber, and fiber-reinforced products.

C17   **SOURCES AND RESOURCES**   Edited By Morton Schlesinger. New York, Textile Information Sources, 1968- . Minimum of nine issues/year. $75/year. From: Textile Information Sources, 152 W. 42nd St., New York, N.Y. 10036.

Provides summaries of papers related to textile wet processing, presented at technical meetings, up to 12 months in advance of publication. Also contains a "Bibliography on Wet-Processing" covering articles from about 250 journals arranged under the following subject headings: Analysis, Testing, and Evaluation; Preparatory Processes; Dyeing; Printing; Finishing; and Miscellaneous. Bibliography is cumulated annually and offered separately to nonsubscribers for $20 per year. Individual issues also include a list of article translations available through *Sources and Resources* and an occasional literature survey.

C18   **TAPPI**   New York, Technical Association of the Pulp and Paper Industry, 1949- . Monthly. $25/year to members, including membership dues.

Some issues list, under "Advance Information," papers being considered for publication. Each listing gives author, affiliation, a brief abstract, and the number of pages. Copies of these papers can be purchased from the *TAPPI* Publications Sales Department for reasonable prices.

C19   **TEXTILE CHEMIST AND COLORIST**   Research Triangle Park, N.C., American Association of Textile Chemists and Colorists,

1969- . Monthly. $3.75/year to members; $7.50/year to non-members.

Advance abstracts of papers to be presented at the annual AATCC meeting are published each year.

C20 **TEXTILE PATENT ABSTRACTS*** Spartanburg, S.C., Technology Services, Inc., 1970- . Weekly. $120/year. From: Technology Services, Inc., P.O. Box 5723, Spartanburg, S.C. 29301.

Abstracts of approximately 100 U.S. textile patents selected from the *Official Gazette of the United States Patent Office* are included in each weekly issue. Abstracts are classified by subject categories: Polymers and Fibers; Fiber Yarn and Filament Processing; Fabric Formation; Dyes, Chemicals, and Finishing, End Uses; and Analysis and Control. Mailed to subscribers a few days after receipt of the *Official Gazette*.

*Discontinued shortly before publication of this *Guide*.

C21 **TEXTILE TECHNOLOGY DIGEST** Charlottesville, Va., Institute of Textile Technology, 1944- . Monthly. $100/year.

Covers approximately 450 textile and related journals, government report listings, trade association publications, industry technical bulletins, and similar publications on a worldwide basis, plus U.S. and British patents. Current issues contain abstracts of about 1,250 documents of which approximately one-third are patents. Abstracts of articles, reports, etc., and patent abstracts are published in separate sections and arranged in these subject categories: Fibers, Yarn Production, Fabric Production, Finishing, Apparel Production, Testing and Measurement, Mill Management, Sciences, and Miscellany. Author index in each issue.

Textile Technology Digest also offers a Selective Dissemination of Information (SDI) service. Each month, a subscriber receives abstracts selected from the *Digest* according to his specific interests. Cost is $50 per year.

C22 **TEXTRACTS** New York, J. B. Goldberg. Monthly. $30/year,

Domestic; $35, Foreign. From: J. B. Goldberg, 225 E. 46th St., New York, N.Y. 10017.

Each issue contains "News Highlights" in headline form and about 50 abstracts, mostly of the journal literature, but including a few U.S. and British patents.

C23　**WOOLCOTT AND COMPANY**　38 Chancery Lane, London, WC2A 1EL, England.

In addition to publishing seven abstract journals in specific fields of biology, this company offers custom patent alerting and abstracting services in all areas of science and technology. Patent watching services cover patents from 31 countries in subject fields specified by clients. The monthly cost of these services is $8 per country per subject class.

C24　**WORLD TEXTILE ABSTRACTS**　Manchester, England, Shirley Institute, 1969- . Semimonthly. $70/year ($60 for direct standing order), plus $3 for surface mail or $29 for air mail.

Covers approximately 600 textile and related journals, government report sources, standards publications, trade association bulletins, industry technical bulletins, and other material on a worldwide basis. Coverage of U.S. and British patents. Abstracts of approximately 250 articles and reports and 175 patents published in each semimonthly issue. Articles, etc., followed by patents, are arranged in 10 subject categories: Fibres: Production and Properties; Yarns: Production and Properties; Fabrics: Production and Properties; Chemical and Finishing Processes; Clothing and Made-Up Goods: Production and Properties, Laundering and Drycleaning; Mill Engineering; Management; Analysis, Testing, and Quality Control; Polymer Science; and Generalities.

The following journals may be valuable current awareness tools for the individual who does not have access to publications with extensive abstracts sections. Examples of periodicals that publish a limited number of titles or abstracts are:

C25 **CHEMICAL AGE** London, Benn Brothers Ltd., 1919- . Bi-weekly. $35/year (airfreight) to U.S. subscribers.
Titles of approximately 120 British patents open to inspection are included in each issue.

C26 **FASERFORSCHUNG UND TEXTILTECHNIK** Berlin, Akademie-Verlag Gmbh, 1950- . Approximately $46/year. In German.
Each issue reviews about 150 European, U.S., and Japanese patents arranged by patent classification. Patent number, title, assignee, date of issue or date open for inspection, International Patent Class, and related data are given. In the regular literature review, titles and references are given for about 200 journal articles, arranged by subject classification.

C27 **INTERNATIONAL DYER** London, Textile Business Press Ltd., 1963- . Semimonthly. Approximately $7.00 per year, plus $2.50 for postage.
Publishes fairly detailed abstracts of seven or eight recent British patents in each issue.

C28 **JOURNAL OF RESEARCH OF THE NATIONAL BUREAU OF STANDARDS, SECTION A: PHYSICS AND CHEMISTRY** Washington, D.C., National Bureau of Standards, 1959- . Bimonthly. $9.50/year, Domestic; $11.75, Foreign.
Abstracts of selected NBS reports and other publications are given in each issue.

C29 **THE KNITTER** Charlotte, N.C., Clark Publishing Co., 1937- . Monthly. Free to major officials of all U.S. and Canadian knitting mills; $6/year to others.
Each issue contains abstracts of about seven U.S. patents related to the knitting industry plus occasional listings of additional patents with number, assignee, and a brief description of the patent subject.

C30 **TEINTEX** Paris, Editions Teintex, 1936- . Monthly. Approximately $16/year. In French.

Each issue contains about 35 abstracts of French patents and articles published in several American, British, and German journals.

C31 **TEXTIL-PRAXIS INTERNATIONAL**   Stuttgart, Germany, Konradin-Verlag Robert Kohlhammer, 1946- . Monthly. Approximately $24/year. In German.

Each issue regularly contains 15 to 20 abstracts of articles appearing in other textile journals.

C32 **TEXTILE MANUFACTURER**   Manchester, England, Emmott and Co. Ltd., 1874- . Monthly. Approximately $17/year.

Abstracts of five or six British patents, selected from the patent specifications, are published in each issue. Listings of more recent patents are also included.

C33 **TEXTILE WORLD**   Atlanta, Ga., McGraw-Hill, 1897- . Monthly. $15/year.

Brief descriptions of new processes, often obtained from British patents, are included in "Textile Chemistry" section.

C34 **TEXTILES CHIMIQUES**   Paris, Comité International de la Rayonne et des Fibres Synthetique, 1951- . Monthly. Approximately $11/year. In French.

Abstracts of about 20 articles from U.S., European, and Japanese journals appear in each issue in classified arrangement. Book reviews also published in some issues.

4

Past Research and Development Results

This chapter presents sources of scientific and technical information which can function as tools for retrospective searching. As such, they enable the researcher to become aware of and benefit from the past literature in his field of interest.

The major keyterm in this discussion is SUBJECT INDEX because it is the most frequently used entrée to the published information in a defined area, in this case, fibers and textiles. Without such indexes, the task of identifying relevant documents, even if abstracts are arranged by subject classification, is both tedious and time-consuming. Several sources previously listed as current awareness services also appear in this chapter, as they provide subject indexes annually or cumulated for several years. Most of these services also publish other kinds of useful annual or cumulated indexes as well. A few publish keyterm indexes which serve the same purpose as subject indexes; many publish author and numerical patent indexes, patent concordances, and others.

Sources of past R&D results take many forms, and the textile industry has its fair share. First—and most obvious—are the abstract journals.

Directly concerned with fibers and textiles are *Textile Technology Digest,* published by the Institute of Textile Technology since 1944, and *World Textile Abstracts,* which Shirley Institute began publishing in 1969 as an expanded version of *Shirley Institute Summary of Current Literature.* The *Summary* originated in 1921 and was the major source for the *Textile Abstracts* section of *Journal of the Textile Institute.* Since 1970, Derwent's *Central Patents Index* has included a *Textiles, Paper* section which provides coverage, on a weekly basis, of textile and related patents from the world's major industrial countries. Other pertinent abstract journals include: *Chemical Abstracts; Abstract Bulletin of the Institute of Paper Chemistry; RAPRA Abstracts;* and *Translations Register-Index.*

Closely related to the abstract journals as retrospective search tools are the primary publications which publish large numbers of abstracts and provide annual subject and—generally—author indexes. Two that deal specifically with textiles are: *Bulletin de l'Institut Textile de France,* which abstracts journal articles and French patents with keyterms, in French; and *Journal of the Society of Dyers and Colourists,* which abstracts textile journals and U.S. and British patents. *Journal of Applied Chemistry and Biotechnology* also publishes an extensive abstracts section which includes many abstracts related to the textile field.

Publications which are essentially indexes also provide the means for searching the past literature. These include indexes to Federal Government abstract publications such as *Index of Patents Issued from the United States Patent Office,* which provides patentee and patent classification indexes to patents abstracted in the weekly *Official Gazette of the United States Patent Office;* the cumulative indexes to *Scientific and Technical Aerospace Reports; Technical Abstract Bulletin Indexes;* and *Government Reports Index* (formerly *U.S. Government Research and Development Reports Index*). In addition, there are two nongovernmental publications which provide indexes to scientific and technical information of value to the textile industry: *Applied Science and Technology Index,* an index to articles in scientific journals arranged under very specific subject headings; and the *Uniterm Index to U.S. Chemical and Chemically Related Patents.* In its printed form, the *Uniterm Index* (see Figure 5) consists of listings of keyterms under which document numbers pertinent to the terms are arrayed—accord-

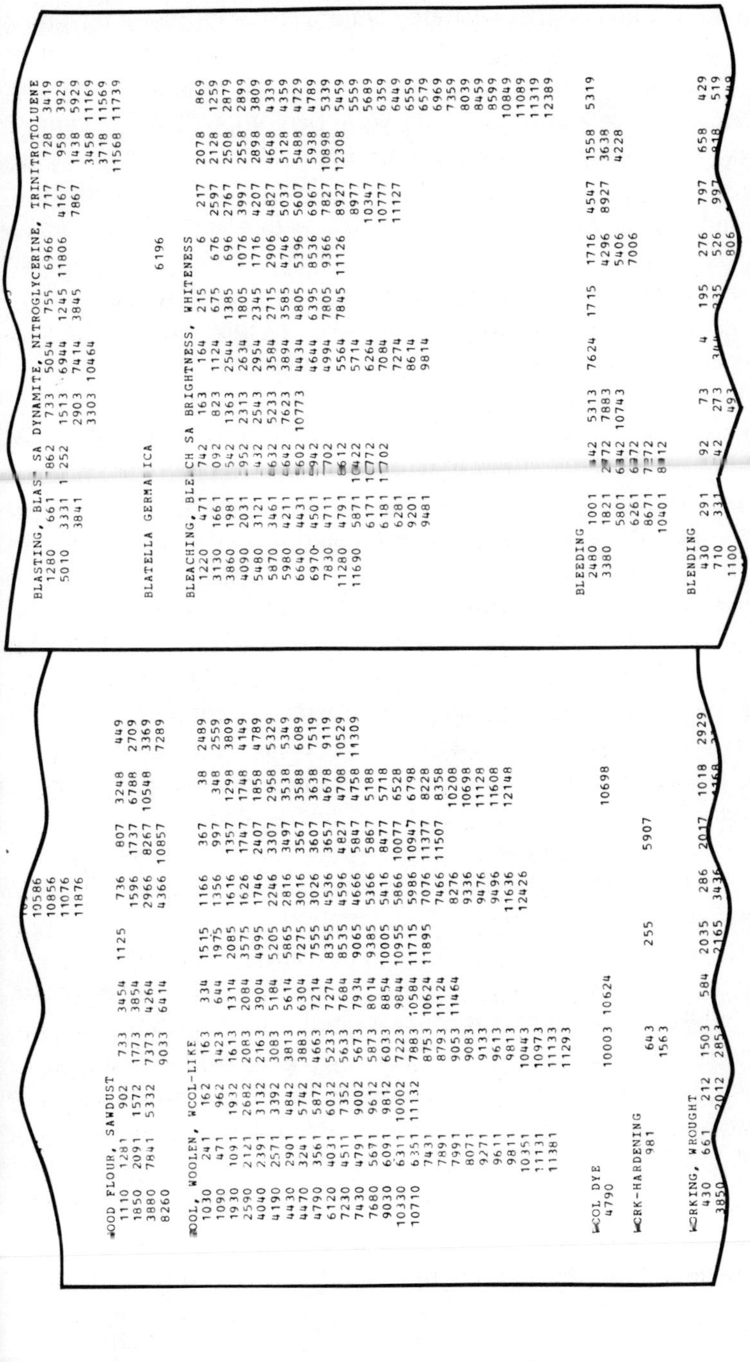

FIGURE 5. Pages from *Uniterm Index to U.S. Chemical and Chemically Related Patents*. Comparing entries under BLEACHING with those under WOOL, seven patents are found to have been indexed with both terms. Listing by terminal digit facilitates comparison.

ing to terminal digit—in 10 separate columns, each representing a digit from 0 to 9. This arrangement facilitates comparison of document numbers appearing under two or more uniterms. Thus, if the researcher is looking for items on bleaching of wool, he compares the document numbers under BLEACHING with those under WOOL. Numbers common to both (e.g., 471) identify patents to which both uniterms have been assigned and which, presumably, deal with bleaching of wool.

Reviews of the literature on a specific topic may take the form of annual bound volumes or journal articles published regularly each year and are very useful retrospective search tools. Current textile review publications are *Textile Progress,* published quarterly by The Textile Institute, and the new annual *Review of Progress in Coloration and Related Topics,* published by The Society of Dyers and Colourists. In addition, the annual volume, *Reports on the Progress of Applied Chemistry,* contains several articles related to textiles each year. Some annual review articles published in textile and related journals are specifically listed in this chapter.

Bibliographies can be another excellent means of locating information on a subject of interest. Some abstract journals list and describe bibliographies as such, or references to them may be found in reviews or surveys. Bibliographies are published in scientific and technical journals and by professional associations and research institutes. Several are included here to illustrate the kinds available and the organizations which publish them.

Much worthwhile information can be gleaned from theses and dissertations which may or may not be in print. *Dissertation Abstracts* publishes abstracts of theses and dissertations provided by a large number of educational institutions, including some that grant advanced degrees in textile chemistry and textile technology. Many other textile schools publish abstracts or lists of theses and dissertations which have been accepted; a number of these sources are listed here.

Thus far, the sources of past R&D results discussed have been those which are provided on the conventional printed page. Some, however, are available in more sophisticated forms. Since 1966, *Textile Technology Digest* has produced a *Keyterm Index*[1] to the abstracts it pub-

---

[1] Merkel, Robert S. "A Computerized Information Retrieval Service." *Textile Bulletin,* 93:36, 38-40, 42-43, May 1967.

lishes (see Figure 6). This is in the same form as the *Uniterm Index*. The *Digest* also offers the same index entries on punched cards or magnetic tapes. *World Textile Abstracts* has recently begun production of magnetic tapes for searching the *Abstracts* data base[2] which covers abstracts published since the beginning of 1970. A unique feature of this data base is the use of characterization codes to describe each document (e.g., review, new work, technical information). Another textile data base now available is TITUS[3] (Textile Information Treatment Users' Service), which is based primarily on keyterm entries for abstracts published in *Bulletin de l'Institut Textile de France* since 1968, but will include additional information in the future.

The textile data base developed at the Massachusetts Institute of Technology under the Textile Information Retrieval Program[4] (TIRP) sponsored by the U.S. Department of Commerce deserves special mention. This is a closed file which was developed to test the on-line information retrieval program. However, it includes documents of lasting interest and, although not updated with entries for current documents, is a valuable source of textile processing information. The data base is available for retrospective searching at North Carolina Science and Technology Research Center (see E15). A machine searching program, not being used at present, will permit the searcher at an on-line terminal to consult its built-in thesaurus, to search forward in time by citations of an author's paper or backward in time through the papers of authors cited in a pertinent document, and to perform other information retrieval feats not permitted by other programs used with textile data bases.

Magnetic tapes are available from Derwent Publications Ltd. for subject searching the *CHEMDOC* and *PLASDOC* sections of the *Central Patents Index*.[5] At present, computer-readable files are not produced

[2] Cumberbirch, R. J. E. and Ellis, K. C. "Computer-Based Textile Information Services." *Textile Institute and Industry*, 9:69-73, March 1971.

[3] "Système International de Documentation Textile Automisèe." *Industrie Textile Belge*, 12:47-48, December 1970. Summary of a presentation by J. M. Ducrot, Director of Documentation, l'Institut Textile de France.

[4] Sheldon, R. C., Roach, R. A., and Backer, S. "Design of an On-Line Computer-Based Textile Information Retrieval System." *Textile Research Journal*, 38:81-100, 1968.

[5] Hyams, M. "Chemical Patents Information." *Chemistry in Britain*, 6:416-420, 1970.

4630
DISPERSANTS
DISPERSE DYES
4830   4841   4042   6623   5885   4836   4337   4338   4339
5630   6631   4832   7163   5437   4588   4829
6030   6602   6617   4828
6610   6622   6578
6620   6632   6648
7150
DISPERSING
DISPERSION
DISPERSIONS

DI LIBRARIES
DI LICKERINS

LIFE   4615
    6510
LIFE TESTING
LIFTERS
DI LIFTING MECHANISMS
LIGHT
DI LIGHTFASTNESS   4561   4832   6623   5474   6846   4337   6177-21
    4370   5751   5442   6943   5704   6966   5437   7177   5378   5479
                                                    6617   5478

LIGHTING
LIGHTING EQUIPMENT   6915   7266
LIGNIN   4015
    4321
LINEAR PROGRAMMING
LINEN SUPPLY NEWS   6862   5663- 8   5664- 3
7165
7175

LINENLIKE CROSS SECTIONS   4436   5558
LINKS-LINKS
                    4202
LINT CLEANERS   5326
LIQUID LEVEL
LIQUID LEVEL CONTROL
LIQUIDS

FIGURE 6. Portions of pages from *Keyterm Index to Textile Technology Digest*. Matching document numbers for DISPERSE DYES and LIGHTFASTNESS indicate that two documents (numbers 4832 and 6623) concern both

for subject searching of the *Textiles, Paper* section, but this possibility is under consideration.

Other computerized systems include: CA Condensates (see C3), POST, and *Uniterm Index to U.S. Chemical and Chemically Related Patents* which can be searched back through 1950.

There are several other excellent sources of past textile information which are no longer published. These are the abstracts section of *Journal of the Textile Institute,* published from 1912 to 1969; *Natural and Synthetic Fibers,* 1954 to 1966, which provided unusually extensive abstracts, often including all the pertinent information of the original document; *Shirley Institute Summary of Current Literature,* available from 1921 to 1968, now continued in expanded form as *World Textile Abstracts;* and *Review of Textile Progress,* published annually from 1949 to 1967, now replaced by *Textile Progress* and *Review of Progress in Coloration and Related Topics.*

The retrospective searching tools mentioned above, in particular the abstracts journals, offer maximum efficiency in covering all major publications in a specific subject field using a single source. However, many of these publications are relatively expensive and may not be available in organizations that are limited either in size or amount of support allocated for information retrieval operations. For the individual without access to these secondary journals, there are alternative, though much less efficient, sources of past R&D results. These are the primary journals which publish annual or cumulative indexes— usually by subject and author—such as the dyeing and finishing publications, *American Dyestuff Reporter, Ciba-Geigy Review,* and *Teintex,* and the general textile journals, *Chemiefasern, Faserforschung und Textiltechnik, Fibre Science and Technology, Journal of the Textile Institute, Journal of the Textile Machinery Society of Japan* (English Edition), *Melliand Textilberichte International, Textil-Industrie, Textil-Praxis, Textile Institute and Industry, Textile Research Journal,* and *Textilveredlung.* Annual indexes also are provided for the polymer journals, *Journal of Applied Polymer Science, Journal of Macromolecular Science, Journal of Polymer Science, Macromolecules, Polymer,* and others. Many other primary journals, not specifically mentioned, also provide annual indexes. A few of those cited above publish a small number of abstracts of articles or patents in each issue and include entries for them in their subject indexes.

Textile Chemist and Colorist provides cumulative keyterm and author indexes to numbered references to articles. *Journal of the Textile Institute* publishes an annual keyterm index in addition to subject and author indexes. These keyterm indexes can be used to identify documents which are listed under two or more keyterms, thereby locating documents more relevant to the search than might be possible with conventional subject indexes.

D1   **ABSTRACT BULLETIN OF THE INSTITUTE OF PAPER CHEMISTRY** Appleton, Wis., Institute of Paper Chemistry, 1930- . Monthly. $75/year to nonmembers; $25/year to academic institutions.

Contents of individual issues are described in C1. Approximately 11,000 abstracts were published in Volume 40 (July 1969-June 1970). Author, subject, and patent number indexes annually.

D2   **ABSTRACTS OF DISSERTATIONS AND THESES** Clemson, S.C., The Graduate School, Clemson University. Biennial. Free.

Includes master's theses in Textile Chemistry.

D3   **ABSTRACTS OF GRADUATE TEXTILE THESES   With an Appendix of Abstracts of Other Graduate Theses Related to Textiles, 1930-1963** Atlanta, Ga., A. French Textile School, Georgia Institute of Technology, 1964. Free.

———— **ABSTRACTS OF GRADUATE TEXTILE THESES 1963-1965** Atlanta, Ga., A. French Textile School, Georgia Institute of Technology, 1966. Free.

D4   **ANALYTICAL ABSTRACTS** London, Society for Analytical Chemistry, 1954- . Monthly. Approximately $78/year, including indexes.

Abstracts more than 350 journals, books, and patents. Nearly 10,000 abstracts published in 1970. Arranged by subject. Organic Chemistry classification includes documents covering the analysis of polymers. Author and subject indexes cumulated for each semiannual volume. Ten-year cumulations also available. Single-sided version available without indexes for $47 per year.

D5 **ANALYTICAL REVIEWS, ANALYSIS OF HIGH POLYMERS** In April issue of *Analytical Chemistry*. Biennial in odd-numbered years.

Reviews analytical methods for chemical and physical properties of acrylics, cellulose, polyacrylonitrile, polyamides, polyesters, polyethers, polyolefins, and other polymers. Techniques covered include infrared and Raman spectrometry, ultraviolet and visible methods, magnetic resonance, mass spectroscopy, x-ray methods, differential thermal analysis, thermogravimetry, and gas chromatography. The April 1971 *Review* lists more than 2,000 references.

D6 **AN ANNOTATED BIBLIOGRAPHY OF COTTON RESEARCH AT THE SOUTHERN UTILIZATION RESEARCH AND DEVELOPMENT DIVISION** By Marie A. Jones. Agricultural Research Service, U.S. Department of Agriculture. Miscellaneous Publication No. 893. Washington, D.C., U.S. Government Printing Office, 1962. $0.55.

Contains approximately 800 abstracts of journal articles, government reports, and patents published from 1941 through 1959. Subjects include structure and properties of cotton, chemical modification and finishing, and mechanical processing of cotton. Subject and author indexes.

D7 **ANNUAL REPORT Textile Research Institute** Princeton, N.J., Textile Research Institute. Free.

Lists doctoral dissertations, related to textiles, accepted by Princeton and other universities. Also includes lists of papers published or presented by the TRI staff and seminars conducted at the Institute.

D8 **APPLIED SCIENCE AND TECHNOLOGY INDEX** New York, H. W. Wilson, 1958- . Monthly except July. Sold on service basis (price depends on number of indexed periodicals subscriber receives).

A cumulative subject index to more than 200 periodicals in the fields of automation, chemistry, earth sciences, engineering, materials, mathematics, and physics. Periodicals covered include many chemistry and chemical engineering journals and a few textile journals. The *Index* lists only bibliographic data, arranged in a detailed subject classification. Monthly issues are cumulated quarterly and annually.

D9 **A BIBLIOGRAPHY ON SOILING OF TEXTILES AND SOIL RE-LEASE FINISHES** New York, American Association of Textile Technologists, 1968. $1. From: AATT Committee on Technology, 642 Fifth Ave., New York, N.Y. 10019.

Contains approximately 100 references to articles and patents published from 1950 to 1968. References are classified under Soil Release, Soil Redeposition, and Soil Repellency.

D10 **BULLETIN DE L'INSTITUT TEXTILE DE FRANCE*** Paris, l'Institut Textile de France, 1947- . Bimonthly. Approximately $25/year. In French.

Abstracts of journal articles and French patents have been published in the *Bulletin* beginning with the first issue. In recent years, between 1,600 and 1,700 abstracts, of which 40 percent cover patents, have been published annually. Subject arrangement and contents of abstracts are described in C2. Annual subject and author indexes include entries for abstracts.

A magnetic tape service, TITUS (Textile Information Treatment Users' Service) became available on a worldwide

---

**Bulletin de l'Institut Textile de France* ceased publication at the end of 1971. The reports formerly published in the *Bulletin* now appear in *Bulletin Scientifique de l'Institut Textile de France*. The abstracts which had been published in the *Bulletin* are now being published in *l'Industrie Textile* (Paris, Editions de l'Industrie Textile, 1884- , monthly, approximately $24/year). These abstracts and the keyterms selected for the documents are still used as input to the Institut's TITUS system.

basis in May 1971. It is based partially on keywords selected for articles and abstracts published in the *Bulletin*, beginning with the 1968 issues. The keywords are taken from the French translation of *Thesaurus of Textile Terms* (see H34), to which some terms have been added. Many other sources are used for the TITUS data base as well, including literature published by fiber producers, dyestuff manufacturers, and textile machinery manufacturers; national or international regulations concerning flammability, fire prevention, and water pollution; and semitechnical information. Magnetic tapes are available for the complete TITUS data base or for portions thereof, selected by time period or interest profile, in a format suitable for the IBM 360 computer. The Institut also offers searching and SDI services.

D11   **CENTRAL PATENTS INDEX (CPI)**   London, Derwent Publications Ltd., 1970- . Weekly. Cumulated quarterly, semiannual, and annual indexes.

Patent documentation service in 12 subject areas that provides *Alerting Bulletins* (see C4) and *Basic Abstracts Journals,* which follow the *Bulletins* by about two weeks and provide more comprehensive abstracts. In some broad subject areas, *Profile Booklets* are also offered, which include abstracts in more specific aspects of the subject. Basic patent abstracts in all of the 12 sections are also available as Company Code Cards for filing by a numerical company code or as Manual Code Cards for filing according to the *Central Patents Index* classification. Basic abstracts and Manual Code Cards for each section also may be obtained on 16-mm microfilm. Complete specifications of patents covered by the *Central Patents Index* may be ordered on microfilm by country or by *CPI* section. Various kinds of cumulated quarterly, semiannual, and annual indexes are available for all sections, and magnetic tapes are available for some sections.

A Punch Code Search Program may be purchased for $575. This can be used with *CHEMDOC* and *PLASDOC* for which appropriate search tapes are offered which permit searching by chemical composition, processes, properties, and uses. A Manual Code Search Program is available for $300. This can be used to search all of *CPI* using manual codes, company codes, *CPI* classification, and *International Patent Classification*.

Derwent Publications Ltd. also provides a bureau searching service for *CPI* subscribers and plans to establish, by January 1, 1973, a World Patent Documentation Centre to serve subscribers and national patent offices.

A weekly *Alerting Index Booklet* for all sections of *CPI* is available for $14 per year, and a semiannual *Alerting Patentee Index*, for $15 per year. Quarterly and annual *Basic Patentee Indexes* are offered for individual sections.

———— **CHEMDOC** London, Derwent Publications Ltd., 1970- . Weekly. Full basic subscription $5,000/year, plus additional fees as illustrated below.

Basic Abstracts Journal, $85 per year. Company Code Cards, $231 per year. Manual Code Cards, $130 per year. *Basic Abstracts* on microfilm, $48 per year. Manual Code Cards on microfilm, $100 per year. Magnetic tapes: Punch Code Search Tapes, $525 per year; Print Tapes, $525 per year. *Basic Patentee Index*, $29 per year. Complete specifications on microfilm, $750 per year.

———— **PLASDOC** London, Derwent Publications Ltd., 1966- . Weekly. Full basic subscription $5,000/year, plus additional fees as illustrated below.

Basic Abstracts Journal, $105 per year. Company Code Cards, $308 per year. Manual Code Cards, $192 per year. *Basic Abstracts* on microfilm, $64 per year. Manual Code Cards on microfilm, $195 per year. Magnetic tapes: Punch Code Search Tapes, $660 per year; Print Tapes, $660 per year. *Basic Patentee Index*, $39 per year. Complete specifications on microfilm, $1,070 per year.

———— **TEXTILES; PAPER** London, Derwent Publications Ltd.,

1970- . Weekly. Full basic subscription $1,250/year, plus additional fees as illustrated below.

Basic Abstracts Journal, $45 per year. Company Code Cards, $154 per year. Manual Code Cards, $96 per year. *Basic Abstracts* on microfilm, $29 per year. Manual Code Cards on microfilm, $78 per year. *Basic Patentee Index,* $16 per year. Complete specifications on microfilm, $590 per year.

D12 **CHEMICAL ABSTRACTS (CA)** Columbus, Ohio, Chemical Abstracts Service of the American Chemical Society, 1907- . Weekly. $2,400/year for abstract issues and volume indexes; $2,300/year for abstract issues only or volume indexes only; qualified teaching institutions may obtain a grant of $500 toward the subscription price.

CA abstracts the world's chemical literature selected from more than 12,000 journals and patents from 26 countries. Approximately 340,000 abstracts are published annually, of which about 10 percent appear in the "Macromolecular Chemistry" section. In weekly abstract issues, the "Biochemistry" and "Organic Chemistry" sections alternate with the "Macromolecular Chemistry," "Applied Chemistry and Chemical Engineering," and "Physical and Analytical Chemistry" sections. For information relating to textile chemistry, the "Macromolecular Chemistry" section is most important. This section covers synthetic high polymers, textiles, dyes, and surfactants.

Each weekly abstract issue contains keyword subject, author, and numerical patent indexes, and a patent concordance. Volume indexes (two volumes per year) include subject, author, and numerical patent indexes, patent concordance, formula index, Registry Number Index, Index of Ring Systems, and Hetero-Atom-in-Context Index. Each year, a guide to using the indexes is published. *Collective Indexes* (decennial and five-year cumulations) are available separately for Volumes 1 through 65 (1907 through 1966). The *8th Collective Index* for Volumes 66 through 75 (1967 through 1971) is now being published at a price of $3,000.

Publication of this *Index* is expected to be complete by the end of 1973.

Subject indexes beginning with Volume 71 (July-December 1969) are available on magnetic tape as CA Integrated Subject File. They are available only in the new Standard Distribution Format.

Chemical Abstracts individual section groupings (Macromolecular Chemistry sections, for example) are available to ACS members for $35 per year, or to nonmembers for $70 per year, with discounts for multiple copies. Each issue contains keyword subject indexes, but the section group subscription does not include volume indexes.

All abstracts published in *Chemical Abstracts* are available on 16-mm microfilm under a lease-subscription. Microfilm for 1907 through 1972 costs $2,200, and $1,550 for each succeeding year thereafter.

Patent Concordance on magnetic tape can be leased for $400 per year, beginning with the 1962 issues. Back issues cost $200 per volume.

D13 **DISSERTATION ABSTRACTS Section B, The Sciences and Engineering** Ann Arbor, Mich., University Microfilms, 1966- Monthly. $45/year.

Publishes abstracts of graduate theses and dissertations provided by more than 160 cooperating institutions, including some colleges and universities which offer advanced degrees in textile fields. Monthly author and subject indexes are cumulated annually.

D14 **ENGINEERING INDEX** New York, Engineering Index, 1928- Monthly. $400/year; $500/year for monthly issues plus annual cumulation. Annual cumulation only, $200/year.

Each issue contains approximately 5,500 abstracts of articles—selected from more than 3,000 journals received by the Engineering Societies Library—and of books, government reports, and other types of documents excluding patents. Journals covered include many on textiles and polymers. Abstracts appear under specific subject headings and subheadings, and an author index is included.

The *Engineering Index* COMPENDEX magnetic tapes are used by many information centers to provide searching services. These information centers include those discussed in E7, E15, E20, and E21.

D15 **GOVERNMENT REPORTS INDEX**   (Formerly *U.S. Government Research and Development Reports Index*) Springfield, Va., National Technical Information Service (formerly Clearinghouse for Federal Scientific and Technical Information), 1965- . Semimonthly. $22/year.

Subject, personal author, corporate author, contract number, and accession/report number indexes to corresponding issues of *Government Reports Announcements* (see B3).

D16 **INDEX OF PATENTS ISSUED FROM THE UNITED STATES PATENT OFFICE** Washington, D.C., U.S. Government Printing Office, 1921- . Annual. Part 1, $11.50; Part 2, $4.50.

Part 1, *List of Patentees*, is an alphabetical list of patentees with cross-references from assignees to patentees. Part 2, *Index to Subjects of Inventions*, is a class-subclass index. A table provides definitions of each class, but the *Manual of Classification, U.S. Patent Office* must be consulted for subclass definitions. Part 2 includes lists of "Libraries Receiving Current Issues of U.S. Patents" and "Depository Libraries Receiving Weekly Issues of the *Official Gazette of the United States Patent Office*" (see C11).

D17 **INDEX TO THESES ACCEPTED FOR HIGHER DEGREES BY THE UNIVERSITIES OF GREAT BRITAIN AND IRELAND AND THE COUNCIL FOR NATIONAL ACADEMIC AWARDS** London, Aslib, 1950- . Annual. Price varies. From: Aslib, 3 Belgrave Sq., London, S.W.1, England.

Sections on "History and Philosophy of Science" and "Engineering and Technology" list many textile theses from Bradford, Glasgow, Leeds, Manchester, and other institutions.

Volume 18, published in 1970, lists 1967-1968 theses. A cumulated edition for 1950 to 1963 theses is available for $169.

D18   **ITT PUBLICATIONS: 1944-1968**   Charlottesville, Va., Institute of Textile Technology, 1969. Free.

Cumulative listing of more than 600 publications including unpublished M.S. and Ph.D. theses accepted by the Institute. Also lists conference manuals, ITT annual and research reports, journal articles, and patents. Author index. Items on this publications list are available on a selective basis within the textile industry.

D19   **JOURNAL OF APPLIED CHEMISTRY AND BIOTECHNOLOGY (Abstracts Section)**   London, Society of Chemical Industry, 1951- . Monthly. $48/year.

Arrangement and contents of abstracts appearing in "Abstracts" section are described in C9. Annual author, subject, and patent (British) indexes to abstracts.

D20   **JOURNAL OF THE SOCIETY OF DYERS AND COLOURISTS (Abstracts Section)**   Bradford, England, The Society of Dyers and Colourists, 1884- . Monthly. Approximately $30/year.

Contents of monthly issues described in C10. In 1971, approximately 2,000 abstracts were published, of which about one-half covered U.S. and British patents. Annual author, subject, and patent number indexes include entries for abstracts.

In addition, *Index to the Original Contributions to the Society's Journal Contained in Volumes 1 to 75 (1884-1959)* is available for approximately $19 from the Journal of the Society of Dyers and Colourists, P.O. Box 244, Perkin House, 82 Grattan Rd., Bradford, BD1 2JB, Yorkshire, England.

D21   **JOURNAL OF THE TEXTILE INSTITUTE (Abstracts Section, 1912-1967) (Textile Abstracts, 1967-1969)**   Manchester, England, The Textile Institute, 1910-1969. Monthly.

Based primarily on *Shirley Institute Summary of Current*

Literature (see D36) and abstract publications of other British research associations. Sources of documents abstracted were 600 to 700 journals, government report listings, trade association and industry publications, and British and U.S. patents. Last volume published (January 1968 through February 1969) contained approximately 7,700 abstracts. Annual author, subject, and British patent indexes in most sections of abstracts.

D22 **THE LIGHTFASTNESS OF DYES: A REVIEW** By Charles H. Giles and Robert B. McKay. *Textile Research Journal, 33:*527-577, 1963.

Discusses the literature on this subject appearing since 1949, when an earlier review was published. Covers the measurement of lightfastness, mechanism of fading of dyes, and factors which influence lightfastness. Lists 230 references. Table of contents.

D23 **LITERATURE SURVEY OF FIBER BLENDING FOR THE YEARS 1952-1963** By Bhupender S. Gupta, John F. Bogdan, and Elliot B. Grover. *The Technology and Chemistry of Textiles,* No. 4, 1964. Published by School of Textiles, North Carolina State University, Raleigh, N.C. 27607.

An annotated bibliography of the literature of fiber blending, arranged in chronological order. Contains abstracts of 182 articles from 54 textile journals, trade publications, and other sources. Author and keyterm indexes to numbered abstracts.

D24 **LOWELL TECHNOLOGICAL INSTITUTE: GRADUATE THESES 1948-1959** In *Bulletin of the Lowell Technological Institute.* Series 62, No. 2. Lowell, Mass., November 1958.

Includes theses related to textiles.

D25 **NATURAL AND SYNTHETIC FIBERS** New York, Interscience Publishers, 1954-1966. Monthly in looseleaf form, cumulated annually in hardback edition.

Worldwide coverage of more than 200 journals and patent sources. Monthly issues averaged about 30 extensive informative abstracts, primarily from English-language, German, and Japanese publications. Subject emphasis on production of fibers, physical and chemical properties of fibers and fiber-forming polymers, and chemical treatment of fibers including dyeing and finishing. Abstracts of foreign-language documents are usually sufficiently detailed to substitute for translations of original sources. Annual author and subject indexes.

D26   **NONWOVEN FABRICS** By Jack Weiner, Lillian Roth, and Vera Pollock. Bibliographic Series Numbers 242-245. Appleton, Wis., The Institute of Paper Chemistry, 1969. Part 1—General and Testing, Properties and Finishing, $10; Part 2—Forming Methods, $17; Part 3—Chemical and Mechanical Bonding, $11; and Part 4—Uses, $8.

An annotated bibliography of articles, patents, and reports concerning the manufacture, properties, and uses of nonwovens. The documents abstracted cover the production of nonwovens on textile machinery and on wet- and dry-papermaking equipment. Each Part has subject, author, and patent indexes.

D27   **POLYMER SCIENCE AND TECHNOLOGY (POST)**   Columbus, Ohio, Chemical Abstracts Service of the American Chemical Society, 1967- . Biweekly. $2,500/year.

See C14 for description of the contents of the POST magnetic tapes.

Information centers which offer retrospective searching services for POST include those listed in E7 and E20.

D28   **PUBLICATIONS AND TITLES OF THESES**   Leeds, England, University of Leeds, 1927- . Annual. Free.

Contains lists of titles of theses accepted for advanced degrees and publications of faculty members.

D29   **RAPRA ABSTRACTS**   Shawbury, England, Rubber and Plastics

Research Association of Great Britain, 1965- . Weekly. $160/ year.

Subject coverage and classified arrangement of abstracts discussed in C16. Approximately 20,000 abstracts were published in 1970, of which about one-half relate to patents. Subject and patent indexes in each issue. Semiannual author, subject, and patent indexes.

D30 **REPORTS ON THE PROGRESS OF APPLIED CHEMISTRY** London, Society of Chemical Industry, 1916- . Annual. Approximately $27.

Usually includes reviews of developments in dyestuffs and dyestuff intermediates; various generic classes of fibers; and bleaching, dyeing, printing, and finishing of textiles. Each section contains a bibliography, and most also contain a list of references. Name and subject indexes.

D31 **RESEARCH AT THE SCHOOL OF TEXTILES, NORTH CAROLINA STATE UNIVERSITY** By the Director of Research. Raleigh, N.C., School of Textiles, North Carolina State University. Annual. Free.

Titles, authors, and supervising faculty members are listed for master's theses accepted. Résumés of results of research projects sponsored by industry, nonprofit organizations, the U.S. Government, and the university are given. Faculty publications and papers are given in an appendix.

D32 **REVIEW OF PROGRESS IN COLORATION AND RELATED TOPICS** Bradford, England, The Society of Dyers and Colourists, 1970- . Annual. Approximately $3 to members; approximately $8 to nonmembers.

Contains critical reviews of developments in dyes, dyeing theory, and techniques of dyeing and printing related to textiles and other substrates. Volume 1, published in 1970, reviews developments from June 1967 to September 1969. Provides coverage of this subject area subsequent to the period covered by the final volume of *Review of Textile Progress* (see

D33). Each article includes references, and there is a subject index.

D33   **REVIEW OF TEXTILE PROGRESS: A Survey of World Literature** Manchester, England, The Textile Institute and The Society of Dyers and Colourists, 1949-1966/67. Annual.

A comprehensive review of developments in the textile industry for the previous year with many references to the worldwide journal, report, and patent literature. Name and subject indexes.

D34   **SAWTRI ANNUAL REPORT** Port Elizabeth, South Africa, South African Wool Textile Research Institute. Free.

Lists unpublished SAWTRI Technical Reports as well as papers by SAWTRI research staff published in local and overseas journals and in the quarterly *SAWTRI Bulletin.*

D35   **SCIENTIFIC AND TECHNICAL AEROSPACE REPORTS (STAR) (Cumulative Indexes)** National Aeronautics and Space Administration. Washington, D.C., U.S. Government Printing Office, 1963- . Quarterly and annually. $30/year.

Subject, personal author, corporate source, contract number, report/accession number, and accession/report number indexes to *STAR* (see B15). Cumulated quarterly and annually.

D36   **SHIRLEY INSTITUTE SUMMARY OF CURRENT LITERATURE** Manchester, England, Cotton, Silk and Man-made Fibres Research Association, 1921-1968. Semimonthly.

Reprinted after a short delay in *Journal of the Textile Institute* (see D21). Continued in expanded form in *World Textile Abstracts* (see D51). Abstracted articles, patents, and other material were selected from more than 400 sources. Last volume (1968) included approximately 6,000 abstracts. Annual author and subject indexes and numerical patent index to British patents.

D37 **A STATE OF THE ART OF DYEING POLYAMIDES: BIBLIOG-
RAPHY, 1954-1965** By Joanne Butterworth, Dorothy L. Gordy,
and William L. Hyden. *American Dyestuff Reporter*, 55:989-
991, 1966.

Lists references for 136 articles from about 40 journals
related to dyeing mechanisms and processes for nylon and
nylon blends. Contains keyterm index to numbered references.

D38 **SURVEY: DYES AND CHEMICALS** In July issue of *International Dyer*.

Published in three parts: "Developments in Dyes and Dyeing," which discusses new procedures for dyeing natural and
manmade fibers; "A Guide to New Dyes," which lists new
dyes and pigments alphabetically; and "A Guide to New Textile Auxiliaries," which is an alphabetical list of new textile
chemicals and auxiliaries.

D39 **A SURVEY OF THE LITERATURE AND PATENTS RELATING TO
BULKED CONTINUOUS-FILAMENT YARNS** By E. A. Hutton
and W. J. Morris. Shirley Institute Pamphlet No. 81. Manchester, England, Shirley Institute, 1963. $3.

Discusses articles, books, conference reports, and patents
related to false twisting, stuffer-box crimping, edge crimping,
and air texturing of continuous filament yarns; the subsequent processing of the bulked yarns; and the properties of the
yarns and fabrics containing them. Covers the published
literature to mid-1962. Several hundred documents are ref-
erenced or described.

D40 **TECHNICAL ABSTRACT BULLETIN INDEXES** Alexandria, Va.,
Defense Documentation Center, 1953- . Semimonthly. Free
to qualified DDC users.

Corporate author-monitoring agency, subject, personal author, contract number, report number, and release authority
indexes to *Technical Abstract Bulletin* (see D10). Cumulated
quarterly and annually.

D41   **TECHNICAL MANUAL OF THE AMERICAN ASSOCIATION OF TEXTILE CHEMISTS AND COLORISTS**   Research Triangle Park, N.C., The American Association of Textile Chemists and Colorists, 1969- . Annual. $10 to members; $15 to nonmembers.

This is one of three publications (with *Products* and *A Directory of Members of the American Association of Textile Chemists and Colorists*) which replaces the earlier *Technical Manual* issued from 1923 through 1968. The Bibliography section has been included since 1955.

Part C of the present *Technical Manual* is a bibliography of articles published in the previous year and books published in the previous 20 years. Numbered citations for articles are listed alphabetically by authors and referred to by number in the accompanying subject index. Articles are classified under headings such as Analytical Methods, Bibliographies, Fundamental Research, General or Historical, Machinery and Equipment, or Reviews. In the 1970 edition, approximately 1,600 articles were cited relating to the properties of fibers, their dyeing, finishing, and uses; and about 500 books were included, arranged in 10 broad subject classifications.

D42   **TECHNICAL TRANSLATIONS**   Springfield, Va., Clearinghouse for Federal Scientific and Technical Information (now National Technical Information Service), 1959-1967. Semimonthly.

Listed translations received by National Translations Center, by COSATI classification, in which Fibers and Textiles is a subheading under Materials. Semimonthly issues contained author, journal, and accession/report number indexes. Indexes cumulated for each semiannual volume.

This publication is now continued as *Translations Register-Index* (see D48).

D43   **TEXTILE INFORMATION SYSTEM (TIS)**   Cambridge, Mass., Massachusetts Institute of Technology.

Originally, this magnetic tape file was used to demonstrate the capabilities of the Textile Information Retrieval Program (TIRP) developed by Dr. Stanley Backer and coworkers at

MIT. It contains index entries for abstracts on textile wet processing, published in the *Journal of the Society of Dyers and Colourists* from 1963 through 1967, and on dry processing (opening, carding, drafting, spinning, twisting, and winding) from the *Journal of the Textile Institute* for the period 1950 through 1964. Approximately 11,000 documents were entered in the file, which is not being updated. It is available at North Carolina Science and Technology Research Center (NCSTRC) (see E15) for retrospective searching.

TIRP is a sophisticated system in which links and roles were used in indexing. The program operates in a conversational mode. The MIT *Thesaurus of Textile Terms* (see H34) was developed for use in indexing and is a part of the information retrieval program. At NCSTRC, the index entries have been converted to an inverted file, which is searched using conventional Boolean logic techniques.

D44 **TEXTILE PROGRESS A Critical Appreciation of Recent Developments** Manchester, England, The Textile Institute, 1969- . Quarterly. Approximately $62/year, including subscriptions to *Journal of the Textile Institute* and *Textile Institute and Industry*.

Most issues contain one or two comprehensive reviews written by experts on the subject, with several hundred references. Name and subject indexes with each issue.

D45 **TEXTILE RESEARCH ACHIEVEMENTS** By J. B. Goldberg. In January and February issues of *Textile Industries*.

This annual review has been a regular feature of *Textile Industries* since 1959. It covers the previous year's significant research advances in manmade fibers and yarns, manufacturing methods, new equipment, preparation, dyeing, finishing, new fabrics, and textile testing.

D46 **TEXTILE TECHNOLOGY DIGEST** Charlottesville, Va., Institute of Textile Technology, 1944- . Monthly. $100/year.

See C21 for description of contents. Volume 28 (1971) contained 13,500 abstracts, of which about one-fourth covered patents. Author index in each issue. Semiannual and annual author, subject, and numerical patent indexes and patent concordance. Although only U.S. and British patents are abstracted, the patent concordance provides information on equivalent patents from many other countries.

Volumes 1 through 24 (1944-1967) are available on microfilm for $54 from University Microfilms, Ann Arbor, Mich. 48106.

Beginning in 1966, keyterms for each abstract have been selected from *Textile Technology Terms* (see H30). Documents are also indexed by source publication and language. These index entries have been published monthly in *Keyterm Indexes* (coordinate indexes in dual dictionary form) (see Figure 6), and cumulated quarterly and annually. *Keyterm Indexes* for the current year are $600, and back issues are available at half price. The same information provided by the *Indexes* (abstract numbers and keyterms) also is offered monthly in punched card format or in serial order on magnetic tape for $900 per year.

Searches will be performed by the *Digest* staff for $15 per professional hour for member mills or $45 per professional hour for nonmember organizations. Output is in the form of copies of abstracts from the *Digest*.

Magnetic tapes for *Textile Technology Digest* also are available for searching at North Carolina Science and Technology Research Center (see E15).

D47 **TITLES OF THESES IN HOME ECONOMICS AND RELATED FIELDS** In March issue of *Journal of Home Economics*.

Theses relating to textiles are listed under: Fibers and Fabrics (properties and qualities, laundering and detergents), Clothing (consumer economics, garment construction and design, production and distribution, historical and cultural aspects, social and psychological aspects), and Teaching of Textiles and Clothing.

D48 **TRANSLATIONS REGISTER-INDEX** Compiled by National Translations Center. Chicago, Special Libraries Association, 1967- . Semimonthly. $50/year.

Replaces *Technical Translations* (see D42) published from
1959 to 1967. Lists new translations received by the National
Translations Center (see E13) from many companies in the
textile industry, with prices for both paper copies and microfilm. Includes classified list of translations, directory of
sources, and index section. Translations of articles, patents,
conference papers, and monographs are listed by COSATI
classification, which includes Fibers and Textiles under Materials heading. Indexes for journal citation, patent citation,
conference papers, and monographs are included in each
issue and cumulated quarterly for the year to date.

D49 **UNITERM INDEX TO U.S. CHEMICAL AND CHEMICALLY RE-
LATED PATENTS** Washington, D.C., IFI/Plenum Data Corporation, 1950- . Bimonthly, continuously cumulated through
the year. $1,950/year.

Keyword entries for approximately 21,000 patents were
added to the *Uniterm Index* in 1970. Included are those relating to the synthesis and use of monomers for fiber-forming
polymers; the polymers and their preparation; the extrusion of
fibers; dyestuff precursors; dyestuffs and finishes; and the
chemical treatment of fibers, yarns, fabrics, and garments.

Book format is in dual dictionary form. Under each uniterm, arranged alphabetically, code numbers of patents to
which the term applies are listed by terminal digits in 10
columns to facilitate comparison for several indexing terms
(see Figure 5). Major terms—used to index at least 10 patents—and minor terms—used to index less than 10 patents—
are in separate sequences. There are approximately 11,000
major and 282,000 minor terms in the book format. Repro-
ductions of abstracts for all indexed patents from the *Official
Gazette of the U.S. Patent Office* are included in each issue
and are arranged by code number. Also included are conventional patentee, assignee, and code number-patent number
indexes.

The *Uniterm Index* in book format, for patents issued from
1950 through 1970, is $5,950. The *Uniterm Index* (exclu-

sive of minor terms) for 1950-1969, on IBM 1401 or 360 magnetic tape, is $17,500. Other cumulated computer-readable products are Assignee tape, Chemical Abstracts Conversion Table tape, Conversion Table tape (code number to U.S. patent number), Vocabulary of Major Chemical Terms, Minor Terms tapes, and World Chemical Patent Index. The latter tape contains foreign equivalents for the top 130 chemical companies throughout the world from 1950 through 1969. Patents are included from the United States, Great Britain, France, Germany, Belgium, and the Netherlands.

Claims of patents in the *Uniterm Index* for 1950-1970 are available on 16-mm film. Microfilm of complete patents is offered on 35-mm film for 1959-1963 patents and on 16-mm film for 1964-1970 patents contained in the *Index*.

Searches are performed in the entire *Index* for $150 per question or on a contract basis (50 searches per year for $4,500) by the *Uniterm Index* staff.

D50   **WOOLCOTT AND COMPANY**   38 Chancery Lane, London, WC2A 1EL, England.

Since 1961, has offered custom searching services in all fields of science and technology. Patent searching services cover 31 countries. Cost of retrospective searches is $8 per working hour.

D51   **WORLD TEXTILE ABSTRACTS**   Manchester, England, Shirley Institute, 1969- . Semimonthly. $70/year ($60 for direct standing order); plus $3/year for surface mail or $29/year for air mail.

Prepared cooperatively by Cotton, Silk and Man-Made Fibres Research Association (Shirley Institute), British Launderers Research Association, Hosiery and Allied Trades Research Association, Scottish Textile Research Association, and Wool Industries Research Association. In part, a continuation of *Shirley Institute Summary of Current Literature* (see D36).

See C24 for a description of contents of semimonthly issues. More than 8,700 abstracts were published in 1971;

about 40 percent were for U.S. and British patents. *WTA* is now publishing at the rate of approximately 10,000 abstracts per year. Annual author, subject, and numerical patent indexes.

Publication available as single-sided version for $77 per year ($67 for direct standing order) plus surface mail or air mail charges. Format permits mounting of individual abstracts on 3 × 5 cards.

Beginning with the 1970 abstracts, each document has been indexed using an authorized *Keyterm List* (see H18) for entry on magnetic tape. Input also includes title, authors, bibliographic citation, language, and a document classification by the following characterization codes: B for books; C for conferences or exhibitions; E for economic information; G for general accounts, superficial surveys, or general descriptions of a subject area; N for new work; O for material that is to be omitted from the computer-based retrieval system because it is trivial, transient, basically advertising, regularly repeated (quarterly statistical reviews), or outside the textile area; P for patents; R for reviews; S for standards; T for technical information; and Z for translations or republications of papers already abstracted. In most cases, indexing is performed on the original documents. Information is stored on magnetic tape in serial order. Magnetic tapes available for $1,000 per year, plus $250 per year for semimonthly updating, or $125 per year for monthly updating. The *World Textile Abstracts* magnetic tapes for 1970 and 1971 are available at North Carolina Science and Technology Research Center (see E15), and 1972 tapes are scheduled for delivery in October 1972.

Starting in January 1972, monthly subject indexes for *World Textile Abstracts* have been offered to subscribers for $33 per year for 12 monthly indexes, or $50 per year for 11 monthly indexes plus annual index (which appears earlier than the regular printed annual index).

5

Major American Libraries and Resource Collections

This chapter focuses on public and textile school libraries, locations of special document collections, information analysis centers, government-sponsored agencies, and similar sources of fiber and textile information. In general, the government-sponsored organizations are charged with the public dissemination of scientific and technical information developed under federal contracts.

The document holdings of the federal information centers and the public libraries are impressive in size and cover a broad spectrum of science and technology, including some subject fields related to fibers and textiles. In contrast, the collections of most of the college and university libraries listed here, while relatively small, concentrate specifically on textile areas.

Large collections which include some fiber and textile holdings may be found at the Defense Documentation Center of the Department of Defense, the Science and Technology Division of the Library of Congress, the Federal Regional Technical Report Centers and Regional Dissemination Centers supported by NASA, and the National Technical Information Service. Other large sources having some textile information are the Engineering Societies Library, Linda Hall Library, MIT Engineering Library, and the Science and Technology Division of the New York Public Library.

The textile school and institute libraries listed here are located at Auburn University, Clemson University, Georgia Institute of Technology, Institute of Textile Technology, Lowell Technological Institute, North Carolina State University, Philadelphia College of Textiles and Science, and Textile Research Institute.

One of the NASA-sponsored Regional Dissemination Centers described in this chapter is of particular significance to the textile industry. This is the North Carolina Science and Technology Research Center which, possibly because of its proximity to the textile industry, has acquired three textile data bases for retrospective searching. Searching services for these textile files can also be obtained through the other Centers in the nationwide network.

The libraries and resource collections included in this chapter represent only a portion of such facilities that exist in the United States. Most of the large fiber producers, textile mills, and dyestuff producers have information centers which vary considerably in the scope and sophistication of the services they provide. For obvious reasons, the services they offer generally are not available to the public. However, some of these organizations do allow outside researchers to use their libraries.

For further information about industrial information centers and other resource collections, the *Directory of Special Libraries and Information Centers* (see A4) and the National Referral Center for Science and Technology (see A13) are recommended.

E1 **ALUMNI MEMORIAL LIBRARY** Lowell Technological Institute, Lowell, Mass. 01854.

More than 32,000 books and 4,000 bound periodicals among library holdings. Includes Olney Collection for which a computer-produced subject catalog is published periodically. Library subscribes to about 500 journals. Interlibrary loan and duplicating services.

E2   **AUBURN UNIVERSITY LIBRARY**   Auburn University, Auburn, Ala. 36830.

Textile holdings are part of the University library. Listings of library holdings and periodicals holdings are issued on an irregular basis.

E3   **THE BURLINGTON TEXTILES LIBRARY**   School of Textiles, North Carolina State University, Raleigh, N.C. 27607.

Library holdings are 6,000 books and 6,000 bound volumes. Library receives approximately 300 current periodicals. Publishes *New Acquisitions List* quarterly and *Periodicals Holdings List* annually. Interlibrary loan and prompt, inexpensive copying services.

E4   **DEFENSE DOCUMENTATION CENTER (DDC)**   Cameron Station, Alexandria, Va. 22314.

The agency of the Department of Defense responsible for processing and supplying scientific and technical reports of Defense-sponsored research, development, test, and evaluation activities. Offers reference and searching services to qualified users. Holdings include about 850,000 technical documents. Maintains Department of Defense *Thesaurus of Engineering and Scientific Terms.* Publishes *Technical Abstract Bulletin Indexes* (see D40). DDC users may obtain documents from the Center free on microfiche or for $3 per document in hard copy.

E5   **ENGINEERING SOCIETIES LIBRARY**   345 E. 47th St., New York, N.Y. 10017.

Holdings of approximately 200,000 volumes. Subject specialties include chemical and mechanical engineering. Offers copying, reference, and contract literature searching services. Open to the public.

E6   **HESSLEIN LIBRARY**   Philadelphia College of Textiles and Science, 3243 School House Lane, Philadelphia, Pa. 19144.

Library collection includes more than 20,000 books and

1,000 bound periodicals. Library subscribes to about 150 journals. Interlibrary loan service.

E7   **IIT RESEARCH INSTITUTE (IITRI) COMPUTER SEARCH CENTER**
10 W. 35th St., Chicago, Ill. 60616.

The Computer Search Center of IITRI has the data bases for CA Condensates, POST, and the COMPENDEX file of *Engineering Index* as well as other computer-readable sources of scientific and technical information. Provides current awareness and retrospective searching services for these systems.

E8   **LIBRARY OF CONGRESS, SCIENCE AND TECHNOLOGY DIVISION** Library of Congress, Annex Building, Fifth Floor, Study Room 103, Washington, D.C. 20540.

Holdings include more than 1.5 million volumes. Offers reference, bibliographic, and consultation services in science and technology to individuals and corporations. Literature searching services also available for an hourly fee. Science Reading Room is open to public. Publishes *Directory of Information Resources in the United States* (see A3).

E9   **LINDA HALL LIBRARY**   5109 Cherry St., Kansas City, Mo. 64110.

More than 300,000 volumes in all fields of science and technology. Especially useful for long runs of journals (including many textile journals) and proceedings and for Oriental scientific journals. Copying and interlibrary loan services.

E10   **MASSACHUSETTS INSTITUTE OF TECHNOLOGY, ENGINEERING LIBRARY**   Building 10, Cambridge, Mass. 02139.

Subject specialties include textiles, materials science and engineering, and mechanical engineering. About 100,000 volumes. Interlibrary loan, copying, and reference services.

E11   **NATIONAL AERONAUTICS AND SPACE ADMINISTRATION (NASA) SCIENTIFIC AND TECHNICAL INFORMATION DIVISION** Washington, D.C. 20546.

Maintains NASA report collections at 11 Federal Regional Technical Report Centers. Prepares bibliographies for NASA personnel and contractors from material abstracted in its publication, *Scientific and Technical Aerospace Reports* (see B15). Also sponsors Regional Dissemination Centers which provide computerized searching services to industry on a fee basis (see E15).

E12 **NATIONAL TECHNICAL INFORMATION SERVICE (NTIS)** (Formerly Clearinghouse for Federal Scientific and Technical Information) 5285 Port Royal Rd., Springfield, Va. 22151.

Stores about 500,000 unclassified, government-sponsored, scientific and technical reports including those for projects sponsored by the Department of Defense. Provides reference and inquiry services to the general public including searches for documents in specific subject areas. Publishes *Government Reports Announcements* (see B3), *Government Reports Index* (see D15), and *Fast Announcement Service* (see C7). Most documents announced in these publications can be purchased from NTIS for $3.00 in hard copy or $0.95 on microfiche. Documents not available through NTIS are noted in these publications.

E13 **NATIONAL TRANSLATIONS CENTER (NTC)** The John Crerar Library, 35 W. 33rd St., Chicago, Ill. 60616.

Provides copies of unpublished translations of material in many fields of science and technology. Receives translations from numerous organizations active in textiles. Compiles the *Translations Register-Index* (see D48).

E14 **NEW YORK PUBLIC LIBRARY, SCIENCE AND TECHNOLOGY DIVISION** Fifth Ave. and 42nd St., New York, N.Y. 10018.

Holdings of more than 400,000 volumes in subjects which include textiles, paper, plastics, and all branches of engineering. Good source of foreign journals. Reference and copying services.

E15 **NORTH CAROLINA SCIENCE AND TECHNOLOGY RESEARCH**

CENTER (NCSTRC)   P.O. Box 12235, Research Triangle Park, N.C. 27709.

Part of a nationwide network of Regional Dissemination Centers sponsored by NASA (see E11), NCSTRC has on-site computer-searchable files for NASA and DDC documents, *Textile Technology Digest* (see D46), *World Textile Abstracts* (see D51), and the MIT Textile Information System (see D43). Through other network centers, NCSTRC has access to the COMPENDEX tapes of *Engineering Index* (see D14), CA Condensates (see C3), *Chemical Titles* (see C5), and others. Retrospective searching services are available, except for *Chemical Titles*. Current awareness services are available for all but the MIT textile file.

The NASA file contains approximately 535,000 documents dating from 1962 and grows at the rate of approximately 70,000 documents per year. About 16 percent of the file is composed of NASA-generated reports, with the remainder being published and unpublished reports relevant to aerospace from worldwide sources. New reports added to this file are abstracted in *STAR* (see B15).

In the Defense Documentation Center file, there are approximately 120,000 unclassified documents collected since 1964.

The *Textile Technology Digest* file is composed of entries for approximately 70,000 articles and patents abstracted in the *Digest* from 1966 to the present. This file grows at the rate of approximately 1,000 indexed documents per month.

The *World Textile Abstracts* file covers approximately 17,000 documents abstracted in 1970 and 1971, and the 1972 file will grow at the rate of approximately 850 indexed documents per month.

The MIT file covers approximately 11,000 articles and patents abstracted in two textile journals. This data base was developed for demonstration purposes and is not updated.

The *Engineering Index* file (COMPENDEX) covers documents from 1968 to the present. Input now includes all material abstracted monthly by *Engineering Index*.

CA Condensates tapes contain entries for approximately 5,000 documents per week abstracted by *Chemical Abstracts* (see D12). Weekly tapes alternate between the Macromolecular Chemistry, Applied Chemistry and Chemical Engineering, and Physical and Analytical Chemistry sections and the Biochemistry and Organic Chemistry Sections. Tapes for *Chemical Titles* are received biweekly and contain KWIC index entries for approximately 5,000 titles per issue from about 650 current journals.

Typical NCSTRC charges to annual subscribers for retrospective searches are: *Textile Technology Digest*, $45 per search; *World Textile Abstracts*, $35 per search; MIT file, $45 per search; NASA file, $75 per search; DDC file, $65 per search; *Engineering Index*, $75 per search; and CA Condensates, $50 base charge plus $5 per volume per section. Prices per profile for a year's current awareness service are: *Textile Technology Digest* (monthly), $120; *World Textile Abstracts* (monthly), $120; NASA file (monthly), $150; DDC file (monthly), $125; *Engineering Index* (monthly), $180; CA Condensates (biweekly), $180; and *Chemical Titles* (biweekly), $200. Documents requested are provided at cost.

Other NASA Regional Dissemination Centers can provide searching services, through NCSTRC, for the textile files, although their charges may vary from those quoted for NCSTRC. They are: Aerospace Research Application Center (ARAC) at Indiana University; Knowledge Availability Systems Center (KASC) at the University of Pittsburgh; New England Research Application Center (NERAC) at the University of Connecticut; Technology Application Center (TAC) at the University of New Mexico; and Western Research Application Center (WESRAC) at the University of Southern California.

E16   **PRICE GILBERT MEMORIAL LIBRARY**   Georgia Institute of Technology, 225 North Ave., N.W., Atlanta, Ga. 30332.

Textiles collection is a part of the Price Gilbert Memorial Library. Interlibrary loan and copying services.

E17 **ROGER MILLIKEN TEXTILE LIBRARY** Textile Information Center, Institute of Textile Technology, Charlottesville, Va. 22902.
Holdings include 7,000 books and 14,000 volumes of periodicals as well as patents, translations, and other material. Library subscribes to about 500 periodicals. Publishes a monthly Library Accessions List which is prepared for member mills of the Institute, but is available on request to other organizations. Library loan and copying services.

E18 **SIRRINE LIBRARY** School of Industrial Management and Textile Science, Clemson University, Clemson, S.C. 29631.
Complete List of All Books in School of Textiles Library (Sirrine Library) was published in 1959. *Additions to Sirrine Library* published on irregular schedule since then. Library loan and copying services.

E19 **TEXTILE RESEARCH INSTITUTE LIBRARY** Textile Research Institute, P.O. Box 625, 601 Prospect Ave., Princeton, N.J. 08540.
Library holdings are 5,000 books and 5,000 bound journals. Current journal subscriptions number about 150. Publishes list of journal holdings two to three times a year. Interlibrary loan and copying services. Open to the public.

E20 **3i COMPANY/INFORMATION INTERSCIENCE INCORPORATED** 8155 Van Nuys Blvd., Van Nuys, Calif. 91402.
This company provides current awareness and retrospective searching services for CA Condensates, *Chemical Titles,* POST, the COMPENDEX tapes of *Engineering Index,* and other scientific data bases.

E21 **UNIVERSITY OF GEORGIA COMPUTER CENTER** Athens, Ga. 30601.
The Computer Center offers current awareness and retrospective searching services for CA Condensates, *Chemical Titles,* the COMPENDEX tapes of *Engineering Index,* and several other data bases. Current awareness searches of CA Con-

densates are $14 per profile per issue for odd *and* even issues or $7 per profile per issue for odd *or* even issues only; retrospective searches cost $75 per volume (odd and even issues) or $40 per volume (odd or even issues only) for each search. For COMPENDEX, current awareness services cost $10 per profile per issue; retrospective searches cost $100 per volume. For *Chemical Titles,* each retrospective search costs $70 per volume. Discounts are given to academic institutions for most services.

E22   **U.S. NATIONAL BUREAU OF STANDARDS LIBRARY**   Route 70S and Quince Orchard Rd., Washington, D.C. 20234 (Gaithersburg, Md. 20760).

Approximately 125,000 volumes in physical sciences, engineering, and technology. Interlibrary loan, reference, and copying services.

E23   **U.S. PATENT OFFICE, SCIENTIFIC LIBRARY**   2111 Jefferson Davis Highway, Arlington, Va. (Washington, D.C. 20231).

Holdings of more than 300,000 volumes. Subjects of special strength are applied science, technology, and patents. Interlibrary loan, reference, and copying services.

6

Handbooks, Encyclopedias, and Other Reference Sources

The listings in this chapter have been selected to illustrate the types of publications which provide valuable reference information and, hopefully, include the most important sources published in recent years. They include handbooks, encyclopedias, dictionaries, collections of papers from symposia, and books which present factual scientific or technical information related to fibers and textiles. For more extensive lists of textile books, encyclopedias, and other useful tools, some of the tertiary sources described in Chapter 1, particularly A6 and A18, should be consulted.

The intention here is to suggest sources for locating information about (1) the materials used in the production of fibers and their properties and (2) the processes and machinery used in fiber production, yarn preparation, knitting, weaving, nonwovens production, dyeing, printing, finishing, analysis, and testing. Although machinery used in textile processes is covered in part by several of the publications listed, no single source deals specifically and comprehensively with the subject. Among the best current sources of machinery information are the reviews of the American Textile Machinery Exhibition-International (ATME-I), held in Greenville, S.C. every two years. These reviews are published regularly in *American Dyestuff Reporter, America's Textile Reporter, Canadian Textile Journal, Modern Textiles, Textile Bulletin, Textile Industries, Textile Manufacturer, Textile Month, Textile News,* and *Textile World,* among others. Also, the reviews of the Knitting Arts Exhibition held in the intervening years in Atlantic City provide information about knitting machinery. Such reviews are published by *The Knitter, Knitting Industries, Knitting Mill Management, Knitting Mill News,* and other textile journals.

The textile standards issued by several organizations which are described in this chapter represent the output of only a small number of the groups involved in such work. Some of the others are the British Standards Association; Canadian Standards Association; Deutscher Normenausschuss, which issues the DIN textile standards often published in major German textile journals; International Bureau for the Standardisation of Man-Made Fibres (BISFA), which publishes *BISFA Rules;* International Organization for Standardization (ISO); National Bureau of Standards of the U.S. Department of Commerce; U.S. Department of Defense; and other organizations of the U.S. Government. More information about organizations which publish textile standards can be found in *A Guide to Sources of Information in the Textile Industry* (see A6).

The publications of fiber, textile, and dyestuff companies—not included in this chapter's directory—also are valuable sources of technical information. The technical bulletins published by most fiber producers generally give information about the physical and chemical properties of their fiber products and instructions for their textile processing, dyeing, and finishing. A few of these companies also issue specifications bulletins which give performance standards required for specific applications of their fibers under their certification programs. Similarly, most of the dyestuff companies publish color cards which provide information about the application of their dyestuffs to appropriate fibers and their fastness properties on these fibers. Usually, they also contain dyed samples illustrating the shades obtained at different dyestuff concentrations.

Other industry publications are: *Fiber Facts,* published biennially since about 1940 by the American Viscose Division of FMC, which gives FTC definitions of generic classes of fibers and a listing of fibers by generic class; *Textile Fibers and Their Properties,* published by Burlington Industries and now in its sixth edition; *Textile Finishing Glossary* from Cone Mills, which has now published four editions; and *A Dictionary of Textile Terms,* issued 10 times since 1944 by Dan River Mills.

The regular publications of the dyestuff companies usually are issued on a monthly, bimonthly, or quarterly schedule. Examples are: *Ciba-Geigy Review* (formerly *Ciba Review),* which originated in 1937 and is published monthly by Ciba-Geigy Co.; *Dye-Chemlines,* a bimonthly issued since 1942 by the Dyes and Textile Chemicals Department of American Cyanamid Company; *Dyes and Chemicals Technical Bulletin,* published irregularly by the Dyestuffs Division of du Pont; and *Palette,* which Sandoz Ltd. has issued quarterly since 1959.

Although this *Guide* is directed to scientific and technical information, commercial information—which is frequently statistical in nature —is very important to the market-oriented textile industry. Consequently, it seems appropriate to make brief mention of several sources of commercial statistics. A recent U.S. Government publication, *Sources of Statistical Data: Textiles and Apparel,* describes federal and other sources and is available from the Superintendent of Documents, U.S. Government Printing Office for $0.40. In addition, many trade associations publish statistics of textile products consumption and production. Among them are: American Apparel Manufacturers Association which issues *Focus—An Economic Profile of the Apparel Industry* approximately once a year; American Textile Manufacturers Institute which publishes *Textile Hi-Lights* quarterly with monthly supplements and *Textile Trends* weekly; Man-Made Fiber Producers Association which issues *Man-Made Fiber Fact Book* annually; National Cotton Council of America which publishes *Cotton Counts Its Customers* and *The Economic Outlook for U.S. Cotton* each year; and The Wool Bureau, the U.S. arm of the International Wool Secretariat, which publishes *Consumer Apparel Expenditures* approximately every two years and *Wool's Percent of Clothing Produced in Specified Clothing Items* annually. Other excellent sources of textile statistics are *Textile Organon,* published monthly since 1930 by the Textile Economics Bureau and *Industrial Fibres,* issued annually by the Commonwealth Secretariat.

F1 **ADVANCED KNITTING PRINCIPLES** Edited by C. Reichman. New York, National Knitted Outerwear Association, 1965. $7.50.

Describes warp and weft knit structures and knitting technology.

F2 **AMERICAN COTTON HANDBOOK** Edited by Dame S. Hamby. 3rd Edition. New York, Interscience Publishers, 1965-1966. 2 Vols. Vol. 1, $16.50; Vol. 2, $22.00.

Volume 1 discusses cotton structure and classification and describes the production of cotton yarns from harvesting and ginning through opening, picking, carding, combing, drawing, roving, spinning, winding, and twisting. Volume 2 covers warping, weaving, knitting, bleaching, dyeing, printing, finishing, chemical modification, and physical and chemical testing. Processing details and machinery are emphasized. Subject index in each volume; cumulated index in Volume 2.

F3 **AMERICAN FABRICS ENCYCLOPEDIA OF TEXTILES** 2nd Edition. Englewood Cliffs, N.J., Prentice-Hall, 1972. $35.

Prepared by the editors of _American Fabrics_. Emphasis is on history, art, and design of textiles. Contains many glossaries and a dictionary of textile terms. Subject index.

F4 **ANALYTICAL METHODS FOR A TEXTILE LABORATORY** Edited by J. W. Weaver. 2nd Edition. Research Triangle Park, N.C., American Association of Textile Chemists and Colorists, 1968. AATCC Monograph Number 3. $15.

Describes test methods including chromatography, absorption spectroscopy, and thermoanalytical methods for identifying textile chemicals, finishes, dyes, and fibers. Many references. General index and index of specific tests.

F5 **BOOK OF ASTM STANDARDS** Philadelphia, Pa., American Society for Testing and Materials, 1916- . Annual. Part 24: Textile Materials—Yarns, Fabrics, and General Methods, $24; Part 25: Textile Materials—Fiber and Zippers; High Modulus Fibers, $22.

Part 24 gives general standards for yarns and fabrics and some standards dealing with specific fabrics including felts, nonwovens, floor coverings, and tire cord fabrics. Part 25 covers general methods for testing fibers and specific standards for cotton, wool, and manmade fibers, as well as for yarns and fabrics made from asbestos and leaf, bast, and glass fibers. Standards also are presented for identification and qualitative and quantitative analysis of fibers.

F6 **BULK, STRETCH AND TEXTURE** Manchester, England, The Textile Institute, 1966. Approximately $8.

A compilation of papers presented at the 1966 Annual Conference of the Textile Institute. Covers the structure and properties of air-textured, false-twist textured, and stretch yarns and factors which affect texturing processes.

F7 **CHEMICAL SYNONYMS AND TRADE NAMES; A Dictionary and Commercial Handbook** By William Gardner. 6th Edition. Cleveland, Ohio, CRC Press, 1968. $38.50.

An alphabetical listing of chemical trade names and common names with a brief description of each.

F8 **COLOUR INDEX** 3rd Edition. Bradford, England and Lowell, Mass., The Society of Dyers and Colourists and American Association of Textile Chemists and Colorists, 1971. 5 Vols. $240.

The first three volumes list dyestuffs by their usage numbers (e.g., C. I. Disperse Red 15). Under each usage number, the names of all known commercial dyes of that type as well as methods of applying them, fastness properties, and other information are listed. Volume 4 contains a listing of dyes and intermediates arranged by chemical composition. Volume 5 is an index to Volumes 1 to 4 in which dyes are listed by their commercial names.

———— **ADDITIONS AND AMENDMENTS** Bradford, England, The Society of Dyers and Colourists, 1971- . Quarterly. Approximately $25/year.

Gives additions and amendments to the 3rd edition.

F9 **THE CONDENSED CHEMICAL DICTIONARY** By Gessner G. Hawley. 8th Edition. New York, Reinhold, 1971. $27.50.

A dictionary of chemical names and terms, including many trade names. Entries give properties, derivation, containers, uses, toxicity, shipping regulations, and numerical code of the manufacturer. Also contains alphabetical list of manufacturers and their addresses.

F10 **COURTAULDS VOCABULARY OF TEXTILE TERMS** London, Courtaulds Ltd., 1964. $5.25.

A glossary of approximately 700 textile terms in English, French, Spanish, German, and Russian. Also includes tables of conversion factors, equivalent yarn counts, and other data in the five languages.

F11 **DICTIONARY OF DYEING AND TEXTILE PRINTING** By H. Blackshaw and R. Brightman. New York, Interscience Publishers, 1961. $5.

Defines terms associated with the application of color to textiles including those for materials, processes, and machinery for dyeing and printing.

F12 **DYEING AND CHEMICAL TECHNOLOGY OF TEXTILE FIBRES** By E. R. Trotman. 4th Edition. London, Charles Griffin and Co. Ltd., 1970. $25.

Discusses the production of natural and manmade fibers, their properties, and uses. Describes scouring, bleaching, dyeing, and some finishing operations. Dyeing machinery, the application of each class of dyes, and dyeing processes for various types of fibers and blends are also covered. An appendix of conversion tables and other data is included. Name, dyestuff, and subject indexes.

F13 **ENCYCLOPEDIA OF CHEMICAL TECHNOLOGY** Edited by Raymond E. Kirk and Donald F. Othmer. 1st Edition. New York, Interscience Publishers, 1947-1956. 15 Vols. Out of print.

Individual sections contributed by authorities in specific subject fields. Considerable attention is given to commercial processes and products, and each section includes a list of references to patents, articles, books, and other publications. Subject index in Volume 15.

A good source of information on the production, properties, and applications of dyes and fibers. Sections dealing with dyes are: Acetate Dyes, Acridine Dyes, Anthraquinone and Related Quinonoid Dyes, Azine Dyes, Azo Dyes, Color (Constitution of Organic Dyes), Cyanine Dyes, Dyes (Application), Dyes (Evaluation), Dyes and Dye Intermediates, Indigoid Dyes, Ketonimine Dyes, Triphenylmethane and Diphenylnaphthylmethane Dyes, Thiazole Dyes, Vat Dyes, Xanthene Dyes, and Wool Dyes.

Fibers are discussed under the headings: Bagasse; Cellulose Derivatives; Cotton; Fibers, Vegetable; Fibers; Textile Fibers, Synthetic; and Wool and Other Hair Fibers. Other sections which relate to textiles include Cellulose, Coated Fabrics, Color (Measurement), Detergency, Dry Cleaning, Fire-Resistant Textiles, Surface-Active Agents, Waterproofing and Water Repellency, and Whitening Agents.

———— FIRST SUPPLEMENT Assistant Editor, Anthony Standen. New York, Interscience Publishers, 1957.

Updates some sections of the *Encyclopedia* and adds the following, relevant to textiles: Dyeing Synthetic Fibers, Paper from Synthetic Fibers, Polymers, and Water Demineralization.

———— SECOND SUPPLEMENT Edited by Anthony Standen. New York, Interscience Publishers, 1960.

Additional subjects covered include: Nonionic Surfactants; Stereoregular and Linear Addition Polymers, Synthesis; and Ultraviolet Absorbers. Contains index to both *Supplements* and alphabetical list of subjects in Volumes 1 through 15 and the *Supplements*.

———— 2ND EDITION Edited by Herman F. Mark, John J. McKetta, Jr., and Donald F. Othmer. New York, Interscience

Publishers, 1963-1970. 22 Vols. $50/Volume; subscription price, $40/Volume.

Continues in the tradition of the first edition and offers many new sections important to textiles—particularly in the areas of finishes and manmade fibers. Index to Volumes 1 through 22 to be published. New subjects covering dyes and pigments are: Dyes, Natural; Dyes, Reactive; Pigments; Polymethine Dyes; Quinoline Dyes; and Sulfur Dyes. Additional sections relating to finishing are: Antistatic Agents; Bleaching Agents; and Brighteners, Optical. Further coverage of natural fibers is given in Linen, and Silk. New sections relating to manmade fibers include: Acetate and Triacetate Fibers; Acrylic and Modacrylic Fibers; Fibers, Man-Made; Inorganic Refractory Fibers; Polyamide Fibers; Polyester Fibers; Rayon; Refractory Fibers; Spandex and Other Elastomeric Fibers; and Vinyon and Related Fibers. Other new sections are: Laundering, Poromeric Materials, Pulp, Textile Testing, and Tire Cords.

———— SUPPLEMENT VOLUME   Edited by Herman F. Mark, John J. McKetta, Jr., and Donald F. Othmer. New York, Interscience Publishers, 1971. $50.

New sections appearing in the *Supplement* include: Carbon Fibers, Phenolic Fibers, Polypropylene Fibers, and Textile Technology.

F14   **ENCYCLOPEDIA OF POLYMER SCIENCE AND TECHNOLOGY** Edited by Herman F. Mark, Norman G. Gaylord, and Norbert M. Bikales. New York, Interscience Publishers, 1964-1971. 15 Vols. $50/Volume; subscription price, $40/Volume.

Format and emphasis on commercial processes and products are similar to those of *Encyclopedia of Chemical Technology* (see F13).

Gives extensive coverage of manmade fibers and includes sections relating to textile processing, yarns, and fabrics. Sections covering natural and manmade fibers are: Acrylic Fibers; Anidex Fibers; Bagasse; Cellulose Esters, Organic; Cotton; Fibers; Fibers, Elastomeric; Fibers, Identification; Fibers,

Inorganic; Fibers, Vegetable; Keratin; Man-Made Fibers, Manufacture; Modacrylic Fibers; Olefin Fibers; Phenolic Fibers; Polyamide Fibers; Polyester Fibers; Rayon; Silk; and Wool. Dyes and pigments and dyeing and finishing are described in: Bleaching; Brighteners, Optical; Antistatic Agents; Crease Resistance; Dyeing; Dyes; Finishing; Fire Retardancy; Pigments; and Textile Resins. Other sections which apply to textiles are: Abrasion Resistance; Cellulose; Fabrics, Coated; Leather-Like Materials; Nonwoven Fabrics; Sizing; Textile Processing; and Textured Yarns.

F15   **ENCYCLOPEDIA OF SURFACE-ACTIVE AGENTS**   By J. P. Sisley. Translated by P. J. Wood. New York, Chemical Publishing Co., 1952-1964. 2 Vols. Vol. 1, $15.00; Vol. 2, $16.50.

Volume 1 discusses the classification of surface-active agents and lists common surface-active agents alphabetically with a description of the chemical nature, uses, and manufacturer of each product. Volume 2 contains information on additional surface-active agents.

F16   **ESSENTIAL FIBER CHEMISTRY**   By Mary E. Carter. New York, Marcel Dekker, 1971. $19.75.

Each chapter describes the chemical and physical properties of a major fiber class and chemical modifications to improve such properties as dyeability or light stability, as well as physical changes designed to improve abrasion resistance or other mechanical properties. The fiber types included are cotton, rayon, cellulose acetate (and cellulose triacetate), wool, nylon (66, 6, and others), acrylic, polyester, polyolefin (polyethylene and polypropylene), spandex, and glass fibers. Numerous references to the journal literature, books, and patents for each chapter. Author and subject indexes.

F17   **FAIRCHILD'S DICTIONARY OF TEXTILES**   Edited by Isabel B. Wingate. New York, Fairchild Publications, 1967. $35.

Provides definitions for fibers, fabrics, finishes, textile processes, and machinery and includes many trade names.

F18   **FIBRE STRUCTURE** Edited by J. W. S. Hearle and R. H. Peters. London, Butterworth, 1963. $35.

Discusses fine structure and surface structure of polymers which constitute natural and manmade fibers and describes the effects of these properties on fibers and their uses.

F19   **FIBRES, PLASTICS, AND RUBBERS* A Handbook of Common Polymers** By W. J. Roff. New York, Academic Press, 1956. $10.

Consists of two sets of tables, one giving physical and chemical properties of individual natural and synthetic polymers, and the second, ranking polymers by their values for specific properties. Includes information for many fiber-forming polymers. Combined name and subject index.

*This book has been replaced by *Handbook of Common Polymers* compiled by W. T. Roff and J. R. Scott with the assistance of J. Pacitti (Cleveland, CRC Press, 1971, $38.50). The new book is arranged in the same order as the former; covers fibers, films, plastics, and rubbers; and has author, trade name, and subject indexes.

F20   **FIBRES FROM SYNTHETIC POLYMERS** Edited by Rowland Hill. New York, Elsevier Publishing, 1953. Out of print.

Describes the synthesis of fiber-forming polymers including polyamides (nylon 6, 66, 610, 11, etc.), polyesters, acrylics, polyvinyl chloride, polyvinylidene chloride, polyethylene, polyurethanes, and others (polyethers, polyimides, etc.); the molecular weight, fine structure, and thermal properties of fiber-forming polymers; solubility, melt spinning, wet spinning, and dry spinning of fibers; fiber properties; and uses. Author and subject indexes.

F21   **GUIDEBOOK TO MAN-MADE TEXTILE FIBERS AND TEXTURED YARNS OF THE WORLD** By Adeline A. Dembeck. 3rd Edition. New York, United Piece Dye Works, 1969. $10.

Contains "Alphabetical Trademark Index" which gives Federal Trade Commission generic classification, brief description, and manufacturer; "Generic Classification of Trademarks" in which fibers—including specific types—are arranged by FTC generic class, a description is given of each, and manufacturers are listed (including fibers not assigned an FTC generic classification); "Licensed Texturing Processes and Trademarks" which describes the process and lists the licensor; "Producer-Designed Yarns for Texturing Processes" which gives the generic class, a description of the yarn, and the manufacturer; "Processor Trademarks of Textured Yarns" giving generic class, description, and manufacturer; and addresses of processors and licensees for textured yarns and manufacturers of fibers and yarns for texturing.

F22   **HANDBOOK OF MATERIAL TRADE NAMES**   By O. T. Zimmerman and Irvin Lavine. Dover, N.H., Industrial Research Service, 1953. $20.

Contains descriptions of more than 15,000 products manufactured by 1,500 companies. Trade name listings give a description of the product, its uses, and manufacturer. "Classification" section lists trade names of products by use. "Directory" section gives names and addresses of manufacturers and the products they manufacture.

———— **SUPPLEMENT I**   By O. T. Zimmerman and Irvin Lavine. Dover, N.H., Industrial Research Service, 1956. $12.50.

Covers new products available since publication of original handbook. Includes a listing of "Products Withdrawn from the Market."

———— **SUPPLEMENT II**   By O. T. Zimmerman and Irvin Lavine. Dover, N.H., Industrial Research Service, 1957. $15.

Contains descriptions of additional new products. Also provides changes in company names and addresses.

———— **SUPPLEMENT III**   By O. T. Zimmerman and Irvin Lavine. Dover, N.H., Industrial Research Service, 1960. $16.

———— **SUPPLEMENT IV**   By O. T. Zimmerman and Irvin Lavine. Dover, N.H., Industrial Research Service, 1965. $21.

F23   **A HANDBOOK OF TEXTILE DYEING AND PRINTING**   By A. J. Hall. London, The National Trade Press Ltd., 1955. $5.50.

Discusses textile fibers and dyestuff classes, preparation for dyeing or printing, general principles of dyeing, processes and machinery used in dyeing and printing, textile auxiliaries for dyeing and printing, and fastness properties of dyed and printed materials. Bibliography. General index containing entries for names and subjects.

F24 **HANDBOOK OF TEXTILE FIBERS** Edited by Milton Harris. Washington, D.C., Textile Book Publishers, 1954. $12.50.
A compilation of data on physical and chemical properties of fibers from many sources. Subject index.

F25 **HANDBOOK OF TEXTILE FIBRES** By J. Gordon Cook. 4th Edition. Watford, England, Merrow Publishing Co. Ltd., 1968. 2 Vols. $16.50.
Volume 1, *Natural Fibres*, discusses production, properties, and uses of natural fibers of vegetable, animal, and mineral origin and contains a directory of natural fibers. Volume 2, *Man-Made Fibres*, discusses natural polymer fibers and fibers from synthetic polymers in detail and includes a directory of manmade fibers, in which the generic class and manufacturer are given, and a list of manufacturers and processors.

F26 **HANDBOOK OF TEXTILE TESTING AND QUALITY CONTROL** By Elliot B. Grover and D. S. Hamby. New York, Textile Book Publishers, 1960. $19.50.
Describes physical test methods and calculations for fibers, yarns, and fabrics, and the use of test measurements in quality control. Subject index.

F27 **HANDBOOK OF TWISTING** By Neal A. Truslow. Charlotte, N.C., Clark Publishing Co., 1957. $5.
Covers the measurement, geometry, and effect of twist on strength, dimensional stability, product life, and fabric appearance. Bibliography. Subject index.

F28 **HOSIERY TECHNOLOGY** By H. Wignall. New York, National Knitted Outerwear Association, 1968. $7.50.

Describes hosiery machines and mechanisms, knitting technology, boarding, and dyeing and finishing of hosiery.

F29   **IDENTIFICATION OF TEXTILE MATERIALS**   5th Edition. Manchester, England, Textile Book Publishers, 1969. $9.

Discusses properties of natural and manmade fibers; a scheme of analysis; and the use of infrared spectroscopy, gas chromatography, and differential thermal analysis in the identification of fibers. Includes longitudinal and cross-sectional photomicrographs of the major fiber types. Subject index.

F30   **INDEX TO MANMADE FIBRES OF THE WORLD**   4th Edition. Manchester, England, Textile Business Press Ltd., 1970. $5.

In three parts: Part 1–"Definitions," which gives Federal Trade Commission definitions of all generic classifications; Part 2–"Index," which lists trade names of fibers and textured yarns alphabetically and gives the generic class, description, manufacturer, and country of manufacture; and Part 3–"Addresses" of manufacturers listed in Part 2.

F31   **INDEX TO TEXTILE AUXILIARIES**   Manchester, England, Harlequin Press Ltd., 1967. $5.

Compiled by the technical staff of *International Dyer*. An index to textile chemical products of more than 600 European suppliers (mostly British) and a few U.S. suppliers. In three parts: textile auxiliaries in alphabetical order, textile auxiliaries arranged according to use, and names and addresses of suppliers. Entries for the products give the chemical composition, textile applications, and supplier.

F32   **INTRODUCTION TO FIBRES AND FABRICS Their Manufacture and Properties**   By E. Kornreich. 2nd Edition. London, Heywood Books, 1966. $7.50.

Covers the production of natural and manmade fibers, their structure and properties, processing into yarns and fabrics, dyeing and finishing, end uses, and performance. Subject index.

F33 **AN INTRODUCTION TO MAN-MADE FIBRES**   By S. R. Cockett.
London, Sir Isaac Pitman and Sons Ltd., 1966. $8.40.
Reviews the history of manmade fibers and discusses polymer structure, fiber structure and properties, and processes in
the manufacture of fibers. In chapters on fibers from natural
polymers and from manufactured polymers, flow sheets of the
production process, properties, and uses are given for each
generic fiber type. Trademark and general indexes.

F34 **AN INTRODUCTION TO TEXTILE FINISHING**   By J. T. Marsh.
2nd Edition. London, Chapman and Hall, 1966. $11.50.
Discusses finishing machinery and finishing processes—
primarily for wool and cotton—softening, weighting, deluster-
ing, resin finishing, waterproofing, mothproofing, mildew-
proofing, fireproofing, and other aspects. Bibliography and
name and subject indexes.

F35 **KNITTED FABRIC PRIMER**   By C. Reichman, J. B. Lancashire,
and K. D. Darlington. New York, National Knitted Outerwear
Association, 1967. $15.
Covers basic warp and weft knit stitches, fabric structures,
and knitting processes. Appendixes include warp and weft
knit fabric samples.

F36 **KNITTING DICTIONARY**   Edited by C. Reichman. New York,
National Knitted Outerwear Times, 1966. $7.50.
Defines terms for fibers, yarns, stitches, fabric structures,
knitting machinery, dyeing and finishing, and garment fabri-
cation, with many illustrations. Glossaries for knitting machine models, manufacturers of knitting equipment, and knitting yarn trademarks.

F37 **MAN-MADE FIBERS, Science and Technology**   Edited by H. F.
Mark, S. M. Atlas, and E. Cernia. New York, Interscience Publishers, 1967-1968. 3 Vols. Vol. 1, $17.50; Vol. 2, $19.95; Vol.
3, $27.00.
Updates Hill's classic, *Fibres from Synthetic Polymers* (see

F20), published in 1953. Volume 1 covers the principles of melt spinning, wet spinning, dry spinning, and the morphology of fibers. Volume 2 discusses the production and properties of rayon, acetate, triacetate, nylon 6 and 66 fibers, as well as other nylon fibers including nylon 6-T, MXD-6, 610, and 11. Volume 3 deals with the production and properties of polyester, acrylic, modacrylic, polyvinyl acetate, polyvinyl chloride, polyvinylidene chloride, polyolefin, spandex, glass, and metal fibers and also discusses dyeing, finishing, and fiber testing. Author and subject indexes in Volumes 1 and 2, cumulated for all three in Volume 3.

F38   **MAN-MADE FIBRES** By R. W. Moncrieff. 4th Edition. New York, Wiley, 1963. Revised Impression 1966. $13.95.

Discusses the structure and properties of fibers, fibers from natural and synthetic polymers, and textile processing. For each class of fibers, covers history, chemical nature, manufacturing process, physical and chemical properties, dyeing, and uses, with commercial examples for each class of fibers. Includes list of commercial manmade fibers which gives the type of fiber and the manufacturer. Subject index.

F39   **MAN-MADE TEXTILE ENCYCLOPEDIA** Edited by J. J. Press. New York, Textile Book Publishers, 1959. $25.

Chapters contributed by authorities cover raw materials; fiber manufacture, properties, and identification; textile processing operations; production of fibrous materials for various applications; dyeing and finishing; performance standards for textiles; apparel manufacture; and marketing, economics, and statistics. Includes a glossary of textile terms and a subject index.

F40   **MANUAL OF COTTON SPINNING** New York, Textile Book Publishers, 1964-1965. 5 Vols. Vol. 1, $11; Vol. 2, Part 1– $15, Part 2–$10; Vol. 3, $15; Vol. 4, Part 1–$10, Part 2– $11, Vol. 5, $11.

Prepared under the auspices of The Textile Institute. Volume 1, *Raw Cotton Production and Marketing,* reviews the history and structure of the cotton industry and discusses the growing, harvesting, and ginning of the cotton crop and subsequent marketing. Part 1 of Volume 2, *The Characteristics of Raw Cotton,* discusses morphology, staple length, maturity, fineness, mechanical properties, and grading of cotton; Part 2, *Opening and Cleaning,* describes the principles, practice, and machinery of these processes. Volume 3, *Carding,* covers machinery and processes of carding. Part 1 of Volume 4, *The Principles of Roller Drafting and the Irregularity of Drafted Materials,* describes drafting machinery and processes and discusses the analysis and causes of yarn variability; Part 2, *Drawframes, Combers, and Speedframes,* describes these machines and their operation. Volume 5 covers *The Principles and Theory of Ring Spinning.* Each of the seven parts of this *Manual* contains a subject index, and most also include a name index and list of references or bibliography.

F41   **MANUAL OF MAN-MADE FIBRES   Their Manufacture, Properties, and Identification**   By Charles Z. Carroll-Porczynski. New York, Chemical Publishing Co., 1961. $9.

Includes manufacturing flow charts, physical and chemical properties of inorganic and organic manmade fiber types, and specific fibers of each type. Defines and describes textured yarns and lists textured yarn trademarks. Gives a scheme for chemical identification as well as photomicrographs and x-ray diffraction patterns for manmade fibers. Includes an extensive bibliography of articles and patents on manufacture, properties, processing, and end uses of manmade fibers. Subject index.

F42   **MATTHEW'S TEXTILE FIBERS   Their Physical, Microscopic, and Chemical Properties**   Edited by Herbert R. Mauersberger. 6th Edition. New York, Wiley, 1954. $23.50.

Presents history, production, physical and chemical properties, and uses of natural and manmade fibers, with greater emphasis on natural fibers. Also discusses testing methods for fibers. Subject index.

F43 **McCUTCHEON'S DETERGENTS AND EMULSIFIERS 1971 ANNUAL** Ridgewood, N.J., Allured Publishing Co., 1971. Annual. $9.

Contains an alphabetical listing of trade names giving the manufacturer, chemical class and formula, uses, physical form, concentration, type, and remarks for each commercial product. Similar listings for intermediates and surfactants from Japan. Another listing has detergents and emulsifiers arranged by chemical class.

F44 **MODERN YARN PRODUCTION From Man-Made Fibres** Edited by G. R. Wray. Manchester, England, Columbine Press, 1960. $4.

Compilation of a series of lectures presented at Manchester College of Science and Technology, plus additional material. It deals with tow-to-sliver and tow-to-yarn processes, false twisting, stuffer-box crimping, edge crimping, air texturing, and the use of textured yarns in knit and woven fabrics. Contains lists of fiber and textured yarn trademarks and machinery manufacturers. Subject index.

F45 **NONWOVEN FABRICS** By Francis M. Buresh. New York, Reinhold, 1962. $8.50.

Processes and machinery for manufacturing nonwoven fabrics and their properties and uses are described. The final chapter is made up of brief abstracts of 142 patents on nonwovens. Includes a bibliography and an appendix of the world's producers of nonwoven fabrics. Combined subject and company name index.

F46 **NONWOVEN TEXTILES** Edited by Radko Krcma. Manchester, England, Textile Trade Press, 1962. $9.

Translated from Czechoslovakian. Discusses materials, processes of manufacture, properties, uses, and testing of nonwovens. Includes 292 references.

F47 **PHYSICAL METHODS OF INVESTIGATING TEXTILES** By R.
Meredith and J. W. S. Hearle. New York, Textile Book Publishers, 1959. $13.

Discusses the use of x-ray techniques, infrared spectroscopy, electron microscopy, and optical microscopy in measuring properties of textiles and the measurement of mechanical, thermal, frictional, and optical properties of fibers, yarns, and fabrics. Each chapter includes a list of references. Author and subject indexes.

F48 **POLYMER HANDBOOK** Edited by J. Brandrup and E. H.
Immergut. New York, Interscience Publishers, 1966. $21.

Contains data on polymerization, solid-state properties, solution properties of polymers and physical constants of important polymers, monomers, and solvents. Subject index.

F49 **PREPARATION AND DYEING OF SYNTHETIC FIBERS** By H. U.
Schmidlin, translated by W. Meitner and A. F. Kertess. New York, Chapman and Hall, 1963. $12.

Discusses desizing, scouring, bleaching, heat setting, and other preparatory treatments of manmade fibers. Describes machinery for preparation, heat setting, dyeing, and finishing of stock, yarn, fabrics, and hosiery. The application of dyes to various classes of manmade fibers, singly and in blends with other fibers, is discussed with examples of specific dyestuffs which can be used. Dyestuffs, textile auxiliary products and subject indexes.

F50 **PRINCIPAL PROPERTIES AND MANUFACTURERS OF U.S. MAN-
MADE FIBERS** In a July issue of *America's Textile Reporter*
Physical and chemical properties, methods of identification and applicable dyestuff classes are given for each generic class of fibers. Also provides a directory of U.S. manufacturers of manmade fibers and FTC definitions of generic names for manmade fibers.

F51 **PRINCIPLES OF TEXTILE TESTING** An Introduction to Physical
Methods of Testing Textile Fibers, Yarns, and Fabrics By J. E.

Booth. 3rd Edition. New York, Chemical Publishing Co., 1969. $16.

Methods of measuring physical properties of fibers, yarns, and fabrics; testing instruments; statistics; and sampling are discussed. Name and subject indexes.

F52 **PRODUCTS/71** In a special September issue of *Textile Chemist and Colorist*. Annual. Available separately for $10. From: American Association of Textile Chemists and Colorists, P.O. Box 12215, Research Triangle Park, N.C. 27709.

Until 1969, this was a part of the *Technical Manual of the American Association of Textile Chemists and Colorists*. In Part A of *Products/71*, American-made dyes are listed alphabetically by commercial names and are identified by class of dyes, manufacturer, and *Colour Index* (see F8) generic names. Pigments are identified by RB numbers for pigment components. Part A also contains a list of dyes arranged by *Colour Index* number. Part B has three listings of textile chemicals: alphabetically by trade name, giving the manufacturer; by use; and by manufacturer, giving use and chemical nature.

F53 **PROPERTIES OF THE MANMADE FIBERS** In August issue of *Textile Industries*.

Chemical composition, physical and chemical properties, methods of identification, dye classes used, and other data are given for major classes of manmade fibers, as well as cotton and wool. Also includes a directory of manmade fiber producers throughout the world and a listing of principal trade names of fibers.

F54 **SPINNING IN THE '70S** Edited by P. R. Lord. Watford, England, Merrow Publishing Co. Ltd., 1970. $15.

Based primarily on a series of lectures for a course in "Spinning in the '70s" at the University of Manchester Institute of Science and Technology, but also covers additional material. Discusses short-staple and long-staple spinning, texturing, network yarns, tape yarns, and twistless and self-twist yarns. However, more than half of the book deals with open-end (or break) spinning processes and machinery. List of references and subject index.

F55   **STANDARD HANDBOOK OF TEXTILES**   By A. J. Hall. 7th Edition. London, Iliffe Books Ltd., 1969. $12.50.

Discusses textile fibers and their properties, conversion of fibers into yarns and fabrics, dyeing and finishing, and the care of clothing. Bibliography and combined name and subject index.

F56   **STANDARD METHODS FOR THE DETERMINATION OF THE COLOUR FASTNESS OF TEXTILES**   3rd Edition. Bradford, England, The Society of Dyers and Colourists, 1962. Approximately $7.

Includes test methods for fastness to light, washing, dry cleaning, perspiration, and other fastness properties.

——— **SUPPLEMENT TO STANDARD METHODS FOR THE DETERMINATION OF THE COLOUR FASTNESS OF TEXTILES** Bradford, England, The Society of Dyers and Colourists, 1966. Approximately $3.

F57   **STUDIES IN MODERN YARN PRODUCTION** Manchester, England, The Textile Institute, 1968. Approximately $4.

A series of papers presented at the 1968 Annual Conference of The Textile Institute which discusses new developments in yarn production including open-end spinning, combined-filament yarns, core-spun yarns, automation in cotton spinning, and other related topics.

F58   **SWIRLES HANDBOOK OF BASIC FABRICS** By Frank M. Swirles, Jr. 2nd Edition. Los Angeles, Swirles & Co., 1962. $10.

An illustrated dictionary containing many federal and commercial specifications for fabrics.

F59   **TECHNICAL MANUAL OF THE AMERICAN ASSOCIATION OF TEXTILE CHEMISTS AND COLORISTS** Research Triangle Park, N.C., The American Association of Textile Chemists and Colorists, 1969- . $7.50 to members; $15.00 to nonmembers.

Part B gives AATCC test methods for identification and analysis, fastness properties, physical properties, and biological properties of textiles. ASTM and federal test methods, cited in the AATCC test methods, appear for the first time in the 1970 edition. Special equipment and test materials used in AATCC tests are also listed with suppliers and prices.

The present *Technical Manual* is one of three parts which constituted the *Technical Manual* from 1923 through 1968.

F60   **TECHNICAL AND TRADE DICTIONARY OF TEXTILE TERMS** By Magda Polanyi. 2nd Edition. New York, Pergamon, 1967. $30.

German-English/English-German dictionary of textile terms.

F61   **TEXTILE AUXILIARIES** By J. W. Batty. Oxford, England, Pergamon, 1967. $3.50.

Discusses the chemical processing aids used in connection with woolen, worsted, cotton, flax, and jute spinning; filament-yarn processing; fabric manufacture; and scouring and bleaching. Also covers textile auxiliaries used as levelling, fixing, or stripping agents in dyeing and those used in finishing for improved hand and body and for wash-wear, flameproof, water repellent, antistatic, antisoiling, antibacterial, and shrinkproof properties. Includes brief bibliography and subject index.

F62   **TEXTILE ENGINEERING PROCESSES** Edited by A. H. Nissan. New York, Textile Book Publishers, 1959. $9.25.

Discusses the properties of textile fibers and describes textile processing operations and machinery. Covers spinning on the cotton, woolen, and worsted systems; winding, beaming, and sizing, weaving and knitting; and dyeing and finishing. Subject index.

F63 **TEXTILE FIBERS, YARNS, AND FABRICS   A Comparative Survey of Their Behavior with Special Reference to Wool** By Ernest R. Kaswell. New York, Reinhold, 1953. $11.

Part A describes inherent properties of textiles. Part B discusses the properties of textile structures which are affected by fabric geometry. Compiles published results of measurements of mechanical and physical properties of fibers and textiles.

F64 **TEXTILE FINISHING**   By A. J. Hall. 3rd Edition. London, Heywood Books, 1966. $20.

Describes fabric finishing for modification of appearance and hand, dimensional stability, and improved serviceability. Combined name and subject index.

F65 **TEXTILE TERMS AND DEFINITIONS**   6th Edition. Manchester, England. The Textile Institute, 1970. $10.

Contains approximately 2,000 terms and many illustrations. Thoroughly revised from previous edition in an attempt to standardize selection of terms for inclusion and definitions thereof.

F66 **TEXTILE WORLD MANMADE FIBER CHART**   In July or August issue of *Textile World*. Biennial in even-numbered years.

For each generic class of fibers or for individual fibers in each generic class, the "Manmade Fiber Chart" provides photomicrograph of cross-section, physical and chemical properties, stress-strain curve, and manufacturers.

F67 **TEXTILES**   By Norma Hollen and Jane Saddler. 3rd Edition. New York, Macmillan, 1968. $7.95.

Discusses the production, properties, and uses of natural and manmade fibers; yarns and yarn preparation; and the production, structure, and care of woven and knit fabrics. Appendixes, fabric glossary, and index.

F68 **TEXTILES: Properties and Behavior**   By E. Miller. London, B. T. Batsford Ltd., 1968. $4.50.

Covers fabrics, natural and manmade fibers as foundations of fabrics, yarns, fabric structure, dyeing and finishing, basic fibers (those most commonly used in specific fabrics), and fabrics in use. No index, but a highly detailed table of contents.

F69 **TEXTURED YARN TECHNOLOGY**   Edited by G. D. Wilkinson. Decatur, Ala., Monsanto Textiles Division, 1967. 3 Vols. Vol. 1–*Production, Properties, and Processing;* Vol. 2–*Stretch Yarn Machines;* Vol. 3–*Typical Market Fabrics; Supplement '68.* $30/set.

First two volumes describe processes and machinery for texturing nylon yarns by false twisting, edge crimping, stuffer-box texturing, and air texturing and the subsequent processing of the textured yarns into fabrics and carpets. Volume 3 contains typical fabric samples. *Supplement* provides additional information on stretch yarn machines. Subject index.

F70 **USA STANDARD PERFORMANCE REQUIREMENTS FOR TEXTILE FABRICS (USAS L22-1968)**   New York, U.S.A. Standards Institute, 1968. $6.50. From: U.S.A. Standards Institute, 10 E. 40th St., New York, N.Y. 10016.

Provides standards of performance (colorfastness, shrinkage, strength, etc.) for 68 end uses in womenswear, menswear, and household products. Includes index of test methods used with the standards.

———— **TEST METHODS FOR USE WITH USA STANDARDS L22-1968**   New York, U.S.A. Standards Institute, 1968.

Provides details of some test methods used to evaluate performance of fabrics against L22-1968 standards.

F71 **WARP KNIT ENGINEERING**   By A. Reisfeld. New York, National Knitted Outerwear Association, 1966. $15.

A collection of articles published in *Knitted Outerwear Times* (now *Knitting Times*). 872 references.

F72 **WARP KNITTING TECHNOLOGY**   By D. F. Paling. 2nd Edition. Manchester, England, Columbine Press, 1965. $6.

Describes knitting mechanisms and machinery and knit fabric structures. Subject index.

F73 **WEAVES AND PATTERN DRAFTING** By J. Tovey. New York, Reinhold, 1969. $7.95.

Contents include descriptions of woven fabric structures, their production, and loom modifications. Index.

F74 **WELLINGTON SEARS HANDBOOK OF INDUSTRIAL TEXTILES** By Ernest R. Kaswell. New York, Wellington Sears Co., 1963. $15.

This is a completely new version of the earlier book of the same title which appeared in four editions from 1934 to 1949. It describes the properties of natural and manmade fibers which make them appropriate for industrial uses, industrial fabric constructions and end uses, test methods, and related topics. Bibliography of 135 references and subject index.

F75 **WHITTAKER'S DYEING WITH COAL-TAR DYESTUFFS** By C. C. Silcock and J. L. Ashworth. 6th Edition. New York, Van Nostrand, 1964. $7.50.

Preparation and dyeing of the principal natural and manmade fibers are reviewed in separate chapters. Also discusses dyeing machinery and the evaluation and identification of dyes. Bibliography and author and subject indexes.

F76 **WOOL HANDBOOK** Edited by Werner Von Bergen. 3rd Edition. New York, Interscience Publishers, 1963-1970. 2 Vols. Vol. 1, $25.00; Vol. 2, Part 1–$34.95, Part 2–$34.95.

Volume 1 deals with sheep raising; grading, production, and marketing of wool; and morphology, as well as physical and chemical properties of wool. Part 1 of Volume 2 covers scouring and carbonizing, the processing of wool into yarns on the woolen and worsted systems, and weaving and knitting. Part 2 describes bleaching, dyeing, printing, and finishing; carpet and nonwovens manufacture; physical and chemical testing; and marketing. Subject index to each part.

F77 **WORTERBUCH DER TEXTILINDUSTRIE** Vol. 1–German-English, by Louis De Vries. Vol. 2–English-German, by Louis De Vries and Otto H. Luken. Wiesbaden, Germany, Brandstetter Verlag, 1959-1960. Vol. 1, $6; Vol. 2, $6.

These dictionaries provide definitions for important technical terms associated with textile processing, dyeing and finishing, yarn and fabric construction, and related processes.

F78 **WOVEN CLOTH CONSTRUCTION** By A. T. C. Robinson and R. Marks. Manchester and London, The Textile Institute and Butterworth and Co., 1967. $11.

Discusses types and characteristics of yarns and woven fabric geometry. Describes in detail the construction of various types of woven fabrics with many illustrations. List of 17 references and subject index.

F79 **WOVEN STRETCH AND TEXTURED FABRICS** By Berkeley L. Hathorne. New York, Interscience Publishers, 1964. $11.25.

Describes machinery and processes for false-twist texturing, stuffer-box crimping, edge crimping, and air bulking of yarns and discusses their use and processing in woven fabrics. The final chapter is devoted to patents under which various texturing processes are licensed. Drawings and the major claim are provided for each patent. Subject index includes names of companies concerned with texturing machinery and processes.

The following subject index to the sources listed in this chapter is intended to help those who are not familiar with the textile literature. Some of the books, encyclopedias, and other aids described are quite comprehensive and appear under many subject headings; others are very specific in their coverage and may appear under only one or two headings. Each source is identified in the index only by its directory number—for example, 2 rather than F2.

Subject Index to Chapter 6

BLEACHING   2, 12, 14, 39, 49, 55, 76
CARE OF TEXTILES   39, 55, 67
CHEMICAL TESTING   2, 4, 5, 29, 41, 59, 70, 75, 76
CLASSIFICATION OF DYES   8, 13, 14, 52
CLASSIFICATION OF FINISHES, TEXTILE AUXILIARIES   7, 9, 13, 14, 15,
    22, 31, 43, 52, 61
DYEING   2, 11, 12, 13, 14, 23, 28, 32, 37, 38, 39, 49, 55, 62, 75, 76
FABRIC CONSTRUCTION   3, 35, 67, 68, 73, 74, 78
FIBER STRUCTURE   2, 18, 33, 37, 40, 76
FINISHING   2, 14, 28, 32, 34, 37, 39, 49, 55, 62, 64, 76
GENERIC CLASSIFICATION OF FIBERS   21, 25, 30, 38, 50
GLOSSARIES, DICTIONARIES   3, 10, 11, 17, 36, 39, 60, 65, 67, 77
KNITTING   1, 2, 14, 28, 32, 35, 36, 39, 55, 62, 71, 72, 76
MANMADE FIBER PRODUCTION   13, 14, 16, 20, 32, 33, 37, 38, 39, 41
MANMADE FIBERS, CELLULOSIC   13, 14, 16, 25, 32, 33, 37, 38, 39, 41,
    49, 50, 53, 66
MANMADE FIBERS, NONCELLULOSIC   13, 14, 16, 20, 25, 32, 33, 37,
    38, 39, 41, 49, 50, 53, 66
NATURAL FIBER PRODUCTION   2, 32, 40, 42, 76
NATURAL FIBERS, ANIMAL   13, 14, 16, 25, 32, 34, 42, 76
NATURAL FIBERS, VEGETABLE   2, 13, 14, 16, 25, 32, 34, 40, 42
NONWOVENS   14, 39, 45, 46, 55, 76
PHYSICAL TESTING   2, 5, 13, 26, 37, 46, 47, 51, 56, 59, 70, 76
PRINTING   2, 11, 23, 32, 39, 55, 76
PROPERTIES OF FIBER-FORMING POLYMERS   18, 19, 20, 33, 48
PROPERTIES OF FIBERS, YARN, FABRICS   16, 18, 19, 24, 25, 32, 33, 38,
    40, 41, 42, 50, 53, 55, 63, 66, 67, 74, 76
SPUN YARN PREPARATION   2, 14, 32, 39, 40, 44, 54, 55, 57, 62, 67, 76
STANDARDS, SPECIFICATIONS   5, 39, 58, 70
TEXTILE MACHINERY   2, 12, 23, 28, 34, 45, 49, 54, 62, 69, 72, 73, 75, 79
TEXTURING, TEXTURED YARNS   6, 14, 21, 30, 41, 44, 54, 69, 79
TWISTING   2, 27, 39
WEAVING   2, 14, 32, 55, 62, 73, 76, 79
WINDING   2, 62

7

Sources of Documents

Thus far, this *Guide* has concentrated on sources that provide information taken from the current and past literature, alerting services, or compilations. Although extremely valuable tools for obtaining data in themselves, abstract journals, indexes, compendia, and similar sources—because they summarize or merely cite—often arouse the researcher's interest in acquiring the full text of a primary body of information. Therefore, in this chapter, the emphasis shifts to resources that provide copies of original documents.

Many of the abstract journals previously discussed offer document services for the articles and reports they have summarized. For example, *Textile Technology Digest, World Textile Abstracts,* and *Bulletin de l'Institut Textile de France* provide photocopies of abstracted documents at reasonable costs. The latter two include order forms for copies in each issue. Similarly, copies of patents abstracted in *Central Patents Index* can be obtained by prepaid coupons from Derwent Publications Ltd.

Other sources for obtaining articles published in textile and related journals are the textile school and public libraries which offer copying services (see Chapter 5). *Chemical Abstracts Service Source Index* is an excellent guide to the periodicals collections of these and other types of libraries.

Publications of various federal agencies—abstracted in several formats—are available through associated document services. U.S. patents abstracted in the *Official Gazette* and copies of foreign patents on file can be purchased from the U.S. Patent Office. NASA reports covered by *Scientific and Technical Aerospace Reports* are available to qualified persons through NASA-sponsored Regional Technical Report Centers or Dissemination Centers. Department of Defense R&D reports described in *Technical Abstract Bulletin* may be obtained by qualified individuals from the Defense Documentation Center. Unclassified/unlimited reports listed in *Government Reports Announcements* and *Fast Announcement Service* can be purchased from the National Technical Information Service. NTIS also offers U.S. patents on 16-mm microfilm.

Documents published in foreign languages present special problems for the average monolingual American. The best source of translations is the National Translations Center, which announces new acquisitions in *Translations Register-Index*. In addition, several publications that offer partial or cover-to-cover translations of foreign journals and generally appear about a year after the original foreign-language issue are listed in this chapter. Unfortunately, a few have been discontinued in recent years, but still are of value for reviewing older documents.

Although most document services offer only paper copies, reports of government-sponsored R&D are available from DDC or NTIS on microfiche or in hard copy. U.S. patents also are provided on microfilm as well as in paper copies, and the National Translations Center offers translations on microfilm as well as in hard copy.

G1   **CHEMICAL ABSTRACTS SERVICE SOURCE INDEX**   Columbus, Ohio, Chemical Abstracts Service of the American Chemical Society, 1969. $100.

Formerly called *ACCESS*, this *Index* is a guide to the location of journals, patents, and symposia proceedings of the past 140 years. It contains a directory of about 400 participating libraries (including those of all the major U.S. textile schools) arranged by National Union Catalog (NUC) symbol as well as a directory of publishers and sales agents. Titles are listed in alphabetical order by CODEN (title abbreviation) and are followed by NUC symbols of libraries holding that title and inclusive dates of holdings.

——— **CHEMICAL ABSTRACTS SERVICE SOURCE QUARTERLY** Columbus, Ohio, Chemical Abstracts Service of the American Chemical Society, 1970- . Quarterly. $75/year.

Issued December, March, June, and September as supplements to the *Source Index.* September issue cumulates the three previous *Quarterlies.* For complete information, the *Index* must be used with the subsequent supplements.

G2 **DEFENSE DOCUMENTATION CENTER (DDC)** Cameron Station, Alexandria, Va. 22314.

DDC offers to qualified individuals copies of R&D reports resulting from work sponsored by the Department of Defense. These documents are announced in *Technical Abstract Bulletin* (see B16) and are available free on microfiche or for $3 in paper copy. Collection includes classified/limited distribution reports. Regulations governing distribution of these reports are given in the *Department of Defense Industrial Security Manual,* available for $1.50 from the Superintendent of Documents, U.S. Government Printing Office, Washington, D.C. 20402. Instructions for registering for classified services of DDC are covered by *Registration for Scientific and Technical Information Services of the Department of Defense,* DSAM 4185.3, January 1968.

G3 **NATIONAL AERONAUTICS AND SPACE ADMINISTRATION (NASA) SCIENTIFIC AND TECHNICAL INFORMATION DIVISION** Washington, D.C. 20546.

NASA R&D reports are available through Federal Regional Technical Report Centers and Regional Dissemination Centers (see E15). NASA reports abstracted in *Scientific and Technical Aerospace Reports* (see B15) are available to individuals subject to the same regulations which apply to DDC reports (see G2). Documents are available in paper copy or on microfiche.

G4   **NATIONAL TECHNICAL INFORMATION SERVICE (NTIS)** (Formerly Clearinghouse for Federal Scientific and Technical Information) 5285 Port Royal Rd., Springfield, Va. 22151.

This agency is supported by the U.S. Department of Commerce, National Bureau of Standards, Institute for Applied Technology. Reports of government-sponsored R&D work which are announced in *Government Reports Announcements* (see B3) and *Fast Announcement Service* (see C7) are available from NTIS in hard copy for $3.00 per document or on 4×6 microfiche for $0.95 per document. Purchase may be made by prepaid coupons, check, or money order, but the preferred method is through a deposit account (minimum $25). The accession (or stock) number of the document or title (PB 000 000) and other identifying information must be cited in the order.

U.S. patents on 16-mm microfilm also are available from NTIS. Microfilm of all patents ($895/year) or only General and Mechanical patents ($600/year), Chemical patents ($300/year), or Electrical patents ($400/year) may be purchased.

G5   **NATIONAL TRANSLATIONS CENTER (NTC)**   The John Crerar Library, 35 W. 33rd St., Chicago, Ill. 60616.

Paper or microfilm copies of unpublished translations listed in *Translations Register-Index* (see D48) are offered by NTC (see E13). Price of each translation is given with its abstract in the *Register-Index*. Translations held by NTC are available in the United Kingdom through the National Lending Library of Great Britain. Similarly, translations held by the National Lending Library can be obtained through NTC.

G6   **U.S. COMMISSIONER OF PATENTS**   U.S. Patent Office, Washington, D.C. 20231.

Copies of U.S. and foreign patents may be ordered from the U.S. Patent Office. Newly issued U.S. patents are abstracted weekly in the *Official Gazette of the United States Patent Office* (see C11) and are available for any of the subject categories or subcategories listed in the *Manual of Classification, U.S. Patent Office* (Superintendent of Documents, U.S. Government Printing Office, Washington, D.C. 20402, $11). Purchase may be made for $0.50 per patent through a deposit account or by prepaid coupons. Coupon books (50 coupons for $25) should be ordered from the Commissioner of Patents.

Following are several useful journals which provide partial or cover-to-cover translations of foreign-language textile and related periodicals. Those which are still published are translations from Russian and Japanese. The two which are partial translations of German textile journals, G9 and G12, no longer are published.

G7 **FIBRE CHEMISTRY** London, Consultants Bureau Ltd., 1969-. Bimonthly. $90/year.

Cover-to-cover translation of the Russian journal, *Khimicheskie Volokna*. Issued about a year after original publication.

G8 **JOURNAL OF THE TEXTILE MACHINERY SOCIETY OF JAPAN** Osaka, The Textile Machinery Society of Japan, 1955- . Bimonthly. Approximately $9/year.

English translations of selected articles appearing in earlier editions of *Sen-i Kikai Gakkaishi* (*Journal of the Textile Machinery Society of Japan, Transactions*). Most of the translated articles were published in Japanese within the previous year. Annual author and subject indexes.

G9 **MELLIAND TEXTILE REPORTS** Heidelberg, Melliand Textilberichte KG, 1929-1964. Quarterly.

Contains English translations of some articles published in German in *Melliand Textilberichte* about a year earlier. Author or subject indexes to some volumes.

G10 **POLYMER MECHANICS** New York, Faraday Press, 1965- Bimonthly. $120/year.

Full translation of *Mekhanika Polimerov*, published in Russian. Issue carrying the date of the Russian journal is published about two years later.

G11 **TECHNOLOGY OF THE TEXTILE INDUSTRY U.S.S.R.** Manchester, England, The Textile Institute, 1960- . Bimonthly. Approximately $45/year. Cover-to-cover translation from Russian of *Izvestya V.U.Z. Teknologiya Tekstil'noi Promyshlennosti.* The English translation has the same date as the original and is published a year later.

G12 **TEXTIL-PRAXIS (INTERNATIONAL EDITION)** Stuttgart, Konradin-Verlag Robert Kohlhammer, 1946-1970. Quarterly. Contains English translations of some articles published within the previous year in the German edition of this journal.

In addition to the sources listed above, cover-to-cover translations of three additional journals began publication in January 1972. Available from The Ralph McElroy Co., P.O. Box 7552, Austin, Tex. 78712, these journals are: *Kobunshi Kagaku,* $295 per year; *Melliand Textilberichte International,* $295 per year; and *Textilveredlung,* $165 per year.

8

Organization of Personal Files

Some of the commercial sources discussed in Chapters 3 and 4 which provide the means of retrieving current and past R&D results are highly sophisticated and are operable only by computer. Other services—which also may offer machine-readable forms—provide conventional abstract publications with subject, keyterm, or uniterm indexes which can be used to retrieve information without the aid of electronic equipment.

These services, however, cover a much broader information base than the average textile engineer or research scientist needs. As a result, he amasses a collection of papers and patents which are particularly relevant to his specialized interests. Usually, he has gathered these documents by patiently scanning a large number of the journals which publish in his special field and, more than likely, he "files" them by tossing them in subject folders crowded into a file drawer. When he vaguely recalls a specific article, he searches through one folder after another until he discovers what he wants, after scanning half of his priceless collection of documents.

There are easier ways of learning about documents relevant to one's interests and simpler systems for retrieving documents on specific subjects. The purpose of this chapter, therefore, is to explore the shortcuts one can use in collecting and organizing his own personal files of significant documents.

To learn of recent publications in his area of interest, the R&D employee may be able to rely on his company's current awareness services, or he could subscribe to one or more of the SDI (Selective Dissemination of Information) programs now offered by *Textile Technology Digest* (see C21) and l'Institut Textile de France (see C2), and soon to be offered by *World Textile Abstracts* as Specialized Textile Information services. If these services cannot be obtained, he can scan selected sections of appropriate abstract journals—most of which are arranged by subject—to find documents which may contain useful information. As a last resort, he must continue to scan a number of primary journals in his search for important articles. However, this task is becoming easier. In increasing numbers, the textile journals are providing abstracts with the articles they publish. Making use of these abstracts can save a valuable amount of time in determining whether the document is worth reading. Many examples of primary journals which provide abstracts with each article are listed in this chapter.

Regardless of the method the engineer or research scientist uses to collect documents, he will want to be able to retrieve them quickly and easily. A number of information retrieval systems have been, and are, used for personal document files. The oldest system is probably the subject file. The usefulness of this method is weakened by the fact that a document is usually filed under only one subject, although it may relate to several. For example, an article that discusses the effect of various finishes on the pilling of nylon may be filed only in the "Finishing" folder or under "Finishing" in a card catalog; thus, it never will be retrieved by searching "Nylon" or "Pilling." This problem can be solved by filing copies of the document under each important subject heading. However, this expands the size of the file considerably and, if multiple copies of full-text documents are required, adds greatly to expenditures. *Concept coordination* offers a better solution and is employed in a number of simple, manual, information retrieval systems.

Concept coordination permits the specific identification of documents by coordinating two or more concepts which are represented by subject categories, keywords, or keyterms. With such a system, the article in the previous example could be found by matching document numbers listed under NYLON, FINISHING, and PILLING rather than scanning all the documents filed under these three subjects.

The concept coordination approach to information retrieval is the basic method used in all modern information retrieval operations whether they are computerized or manual. Several mechanisms have been devised for manual concept coordination systems. They include the use of edge-notched cards, Peek-a-boo systems, and Uniterm (or keyword card) systems.

An edge-notched card system uses printed cards containing dedicated notch sites on their edges (see Figure 7). Each edge site contains

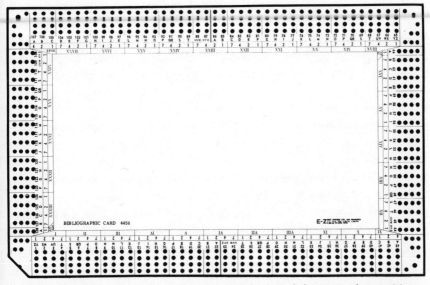

FIGURE 7. A commercially available edge-notched card showing edge positions which correspond to subject categories. Center of the card can be used to provide abstract or bibliographic citation.

a round hole a short distance from the edge of the card and is assigned a keyterm or subject heading. To index a document, a card representing that document (which may have an abstract or only sufficient information to identify its source) is notched in the edge sites corresponding to the keyterms selected. To retrieve documents on a specific subject, the deck of cards is aligned, and a probe is inserted through a hole in the edge site representing the desired keyterm concept. The deck of cards is then lifted; those cards which drop from the deck because they are notched in that keyterm site are indexed by that term. To coordinate with a second term, the cards which have dropped from the deck are aligned again, and the process is repeated. Because of the mechanism of storage and retrieval in an edge-notched card system, the cards do not have to be maintained in a particular sequence. The principal drawback is the limited number of edge sites and, therefore, of keyterms which can be used in indexing.

Peek-a-boo systems use a completely different type of card. Each card represents a keyterm and is printed with a matrix—usually consisting of 100 positions across the card and 100 positions from top to bottom (see Figure 8). Each position in the matrix represents a document number (up to 10,000 on a card with a 100 x 100 matrix). To index a document, the appropriate keyterm cards are removed from the card deck, and a hole is drilled in each one in the matrix position corresponding to the document's number. The cards are then refiled. To retrieve documents, the cards representing the keyterms describing the desired documents are removed from the deck and superimposed in front of a light source. The positions through which light is transmitted identify the numbers of documents indexed by the selected keyterms. For ease in locating cards, the deck is maintained in alphabetical sequence. Probably the greatest deficiencies of this system are the time and the equipment required for drilling the cards to store information.

Edge-notched card and Peek-a-boo systems are described further by Cushing[1] in *Chemical Engineering* and by Nobbs[2] in *TAPPI*.

Perhaps the simplest personal information retrieval system is based on Uniterms as exemplified by the *Textile Technology Digest's Keyterm Index*[3] (see Figure 6) and *Uniterm Index to U.S. Chemical and Chem-*

---

[1] Cushing, Ralph. "Improving Personal Filing Systems." *Chemical Engineering*, 70:73-86, January 7, 1963.

[2] Nobbs, Peter M. "Coordinate Indexing and the Pulp and Paper Thesaurus as Tools in Information Retrieval." *TAPPI*, 48:136A-141A, September 1965.

[3] Merkel, Robert S. "A Computerized Information Retrieval System." *Textile Bulletin*, 93:36, 38-40, 42-43, May 1967.

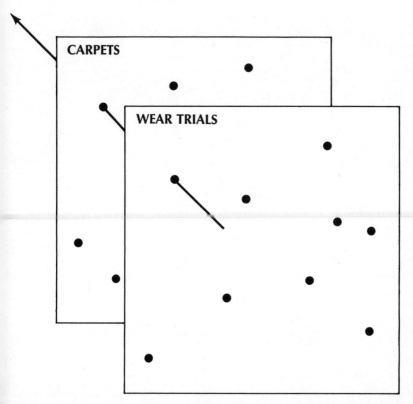

FIGURE 8. Peek-a-boo cards for CARPETS and WEAR TRIALS showing light beam passing through holes in identical positions in the two cards. Documents corresponding to positions through which light is transmitted should provide information on wear trials of carpets.

cally Related Patents (see Figure 5). A Uniterm system consists of keyterm cards with 10 columns, each designated by a digit from 0 through 9. To index a document, appropriate keyterm cards are selected, and the document number is recorded (or posted)—in the column matching that number's last digit—on each of the cards. For retrieval, the cards representing the contents of the desired documents are aligned, and document numbers are matched by column. Those numbers which appear on all the cards identify the pertinent material. The only problem is the need to keep the cards in alphabetical order. An example of the use of keyterm cards is shown in Figure 9. The operation of a personal Uniterm information retrieval system is also described by Cushing[1] and is discussed in connection with textile information by Weaver.[4]

TEXTURED YARNS — GEN-1095 (5-55)

0	1	2	3	4	5	6	7	8	9
20	11	22	13	14	25	36	7	18	29
60	31	62	63	74	85	66	57	48	59
80	81		83	104	125	116	97	88	99
	101		93		135	156	127		119
	131						147		
							167		

CIRCULAR KNITTING — GEN-1095 (5-55)

0	1	2	3	4	5	6*	7	8	9
10	31	2	43	24	15	16	37	18	39
40	71	52	73	54	65	26	87	98	89
110	91	72	123	84	105	66	137	118	159
	111	102		124		136	177	148	
		152		134					
				164					
				174					

FIGURE 9. Manually posted coordinate index (or Uniterm) cards for CIRCULAR KNITTING and TEXTURED YARNS. Matches are found to be documents 31, 66, and 18.

A number of primary journals provide lists of keyterms as well as abstracts for each article they publish. These journals include *Bulletin de l'Institut Textile de France, Journal of Research of the National Bureau of Standards, Journal of the Textile Institute, Materials Research and Standards, TAPPI, Textile Chemist and Colorist,* and *Textile Research Journal.* Examples of keyterm indexing by two textile journals are shown in Figure 10.

Two textile journals go a step beyond keyterm indexing of their

[4] Weaver, W. J. "Information Retrieval for Beginners." *Textile Chemist and Colorist* 1:158-160, 1969.

On the Torsion Constant of Cotton Fibers

C. C. CHENG[1] AND K. E. DUCKETT

Agricultural Experiment Station, University of Tennessee, Knoxville, Tennessee 37916, U. S. A.

ABSTRACT

The measurement of the torsion constant of cotton fibers is usually determined by the single-fiber method. The bundle method proves to be faster, and the determination of this physical property by the bundle method is analyzed and the experimental results are discussed.

KEYWORDS

Cotton (single fibers); cotton (bundle). Twisting; oscillations; number density; linear density; bob weight; inertia moment; tension. Torque; torsional rigidity; stiffness. Torsion constant. Single-fiber method; bundle method.

3—THE MEASUREMENT OF FIBRE ENTANGLEMENT IN SCOURED WOOL

By P. J. KRUGER

An instrument capable of determining the extent of entanglement of scoured wool is described. The results obtained with it correlate well with the carding and combing performance of the wool. Fibre length was found to be directly related to the entanglement reading. A parameter called the entanglement factor is defined to give a measure of the state of entanglement.

KEY WORDS (SPECIFIC TERMS): ENTANGLEMENT FACTOR, FIBRE LENGTH; NOIL PER CENT; FIBRE BREAKAGE; SCOURING, WORSTED CARDING, WORSTED COMBING; ENTANGLEMENT TESTING; ENTANGLEMENTS; SCOURED WOOL, FIBRES; ENTANGLE-METER.

KEY WORDS (BROADER TERMS): FIBRE PROPERTIES; CARDING, COMBING, TESTING; WOOL; TESTING EQUIPMENT.

FIGURE 10. Pages from Textile Research Journal 41: 298 (April 1971), above, and from Journal of the Textile Institute 62: 47 (Jan. 1971), below, illustrating keyword indexing of primary journals.

articles. *Bulletin de l'Institut Textile de France* also publishes keyterms (mots clés) for articles and patents summarized in its "Abstracts" section (see Figure 11). *Textile Chemist and Colorist* enters keyterm selections for articles in a "Key Term Index" appearing in each issue and continuously cumulated through the year (see Figure 12). *Journal of the Textile Institute* publishes an annual keyterm index in the December issue.

Many of the primary journals which provide source indexing (and the abstract services which do keyterm indexing) rely on a thesaurus. An information retrieval thesaurus is an alphabetical keyterm listing that also indicates relationships among the terms (see Figure 13). The relationships are defined as broader term (BT), narrower term (NT), and related term (RT). In addition, the thesaurus may provide USE references to refer the indexer from one keyterm to another that is the accepted term for that concept. Explanatory notes may follow a keyterm to limit or define its use in the context of that thesaurus.

The use of a thesaurus or some other authority for selection of keyterms (keyterm lists, lists of subject headings, etc.) is important in maintaining any information retrieval system (personal or commercial). If keyterms are selected without such "vocabulary control"—probably from the text of the documents—similar material will be dispersed under synonymous or nearly synonymous expressions, indexing inconsistencies will occur, and the index will lose some of its effectiveness as an information retrieval tool. Consequently, the individual who wants to develop a personal information retrieval system is well advised to use a published thesaurus or other authority in selecting keyterms. This keyterm standard should be selected on the basis of its coverage of the terminology of the subject field in which the individual's interests are concentrated.

Many thesauri and other authority lists covering textiles and related fields have been published in recent years. The first edition of *Thesaurus of Textile Terms* was published by MIT in 1966 and was followed by the second edition in 1969. This *Thesaurus* has been translated into French, German, Spanish, Italian, the four Nordic languages, and Japanese. It has been the primary source for the *Keyterm List* used by *World Textile Abstracts* (see D51) in indexing abstracted documents for computerized information retrieval. The French translation is the basic

~~tabl~~ ~~figure. Bibliographie.~~ ~~dans~~

CLIII - 37 563. — WEINER L.I. — The relationship of moisture vapor transmission to the structure of textile fabrics. — Relation entre la transmission de vapeur humide et la structure des tissus. - TEXTILE CHEMIST & COLORIST, Novembre 1970, vol. 2, n° 22, p. 378 (8 pages).

Mots clés : Militaire (Article) — Vêtement — Confort — Vapeur d'eau — Evaporation — Méthode scientifique — Tissu (Structure du) — Modèle mathématique — Equation — Prévision — Mesure — Chaleur (Transfert de).

La permanence du confort thermique par temps froid ou chaud, pour un sujet très actif, dépend de la diffusion de la vapeur d'eau à travers les vêtements et a une grande importance pour les uniformes militaires. Les méthodes de mesure sont basées soit sur la quantité de vapeur produite par une surface d'eau et passant à travers le tissu, soit sur la vapeur de l'atmosphère passant à travers le tissu et retenue par un desséchant. Deux modèles sont proposés, permettant de prévoir la transmission de vapeur en l'exprimant à l'aide des propriétés géométriques du tissu, simples et rapidement déterminées, notamment la densité superficielle et l'épaisseur. La concordance des résultats obtenus, pour des tissus de coton ou de nylon, selon l'équation établie expérimentalement, est très bonne. Quatre tableaux. Huit figures. Bibliographie.

CLIII - 37 564. — ABBOTT N.J. — Wrinkled fabrics, optical illusions and the FRL topometer. — Tissus froissés, illusions d'optique, et le topomètre FRL. - TEXTILE RESEARCH JOURNAL, Novembre 1970, vol. 40, n° 11, p. 1026 (9 pages).

Mots clés : Tissu (En général) — Froissement — Mesure (Instrument de) — Munsell (Système de couleur de) — Vision — Lumière — Laboratoire (Appareil de) — Evaluation.

L'évaluation visuelle du degré de froissement d'un tissu est influencée par le contour de l'article, par sa couleur et sa contexture. Elle est subjective et varie selon les observateurs. Il a été créé un appareil mesurant ce froissement ayant pour base l'échelle de gris de Munsell ; un faisceau lumineux balaie la surface du tissu. On mesure les variations de la lumière incidente. Un tableau. Quatorze figures. Bibliographie.

CLIII - 37 565. — GORJAEV N.N. — Nekotorye svojstva hlopkovinolovyh tkanej. — Quelques propriétés des tissus vinal/coton. - TEXTILNAIA PROMYCHLEN-NOST, Octobre 1970, n° 10, p. 63 (2 pages).

Mots clés : Tissu mixte — Polyvinyle (Alcool de) (Fibre de) — Coton — Proportion — Traction (Contrôle de la résistance à la) — Traction (Propriété résistance à la) — Abrasion (Résistance à l') — Porter (Résistance au) — Porter (Contrôle de la résistance au).

Les tissus de coton et de mélanges vinal/coton (alcool de polyvynile/coton) ont été comparés aux points de vue de la résistance à la traction, la résistance à l'abrasion et au porter (2, 6, 9 et 12 mois). Les mélanges testés sont 75/25, 50/50, 25/75. Les tissus vinal/coton ont des propriétés physico-chimiques sensiblement meilleures que les tissus en pur coton. Un indice de résistance au porter a été déterminé et on montre qu'il est 3,4 fois, 5,8 fois, 11,4 fois supérieur dans le cas des tissus mélangés. Un tableau. Une figure.

CLIII - 37 566. — KOKOSHINSKAJA V.I., ZOLOTNICKAJA K.N., LEBEDE-VA A.V. — Svojstva hlopchatobumazhnyh netkanyh poloten malimo. — Propriétés des non-tissés « Malimo ». - TEXTILNAIA PRO...
~~1970~~

FIGURE 11   Excerpt from Abstracts section of *Bulletin de l'Institut Textile de France* 25: 269 (Mar./Apr. 1971) showing listing of keywords (mots clés) for each abstract.

...2. The compl... index for Vol. 2 was published in Vol. 2, No. 25 (December 16, 1970), p44. Reprints of both are available at $2 each.

The journal is also available on microfilm from University Microfilms, Ann Arbor, Michigan, 48106.

Key Term Index

Index of Titles

In the following Index of Titles the numbers to the right of the entry identify the issue and page number for that article. The digit preceding the hyphen indicates the issue. The digits following the hyphen cite the page number in that issue. Page numbers following the virgule (/) denote continuous pagination for all Vol. 3 technical papers.

(1) Space Treating: A New Version of the Space Dyeing Principle, H. Egli and H. Ulshoefer ...1-31/1

(2) Some Aspects of Textile Finishing, Herman B. Goldstein. ...1-39/8

(3) Rotary Screen Printing Offers Economy and Versatility, Robert Aaron. ...1-45/13

(4) The Effect of Heat Variations in False Twist Texturizing on the Dyeability of Man-Made Fibers, Northern Piedmont Section, AATCC. ...1-47/15

(5) Odor Control in Sodium Chlorite Bleaching, Midwest Section, AATCC. ...1-51/19

(6) How Reliable Are Artificial Light Sources for Predicting Degradation of Textiles by Daylight? A. S. Tweedie, M. T. Mitton and P. Z. Sturgeon ...2-7/22

(7) The Gaseous Formaldehyde/Sulfur Dioxide Durable P...ress. R. Swidler, I...

FIGURE 12. Sections of cumulative Key Term Index from *Textile Chemist and Colorist*, July 1971. Document numbers for two or more terms are compared to identify articles concerned with these subjects.

```
                                    ACIDS

ACETATE FIBERS                      ACID CHLORIDES
    UF   ACETATE                        RT   ACID ANHYDRIDES
         ACETATE RAYON                       ACIDS
    NT   CELACRIMP (TN)                      CHLORINE COMPOUNDS
         CELAFIBRE (TN)
         ESTRON (TN)                ACID DAMAGE
         FIBRCCETA (TN)                 USE ACID DEGRADATION
         LOFTURA (TN)
    BT   CELLULOSE ESTER FIBERS     ACID DEGRADATION
         MAN MADE FIBERS                UF   ACID DAMAGE
    RT   ACETATE DYES                   BT   DEGRADATION
         ACETYLATED COTTON             RT   ACID HYDROLYSIS
         ALKALI CELLULOSE                   CHEMICAL PROPERTIES
         ARTIFICIAL SILK (ARCHAIC)         COPPER NUMBER
         CELLULOSE ACETATE                 DEGRADATION PROPERTIES
         CELLULOSE DERIVATIVES             DEGREE OF POLYMERIZATION
         CELLULOSE ESTERS                  HYDROCCELLULOSE
         CELLULOSE NITRATE                 METHYLENE BLUE NUMBER
         CUPRAMMCNIUM RAYON                REACTIONS (CHEMICAL)
         CYANCETHYLCELLULOSE               TENDERING
         CYCLOSET YARNS (TN)               VISCCSITY
         TRIACETATE FIBERS
         VISCCSE RAYON              ACID DYEING
                                        BT   DYEING (BY DYE CLASSES)
ACETATE RAYON                           RT   ACID DYES
    USE ACETATE FIBERS                       ACID SHOCK METHOD
                                             ANIONIC SITES
ACETATE SALTS                                AZOIC DYEING
    NT   MERCURIC ACETATE                    BASIC DYEING
         POTASSIUM ACETATE                   DIRECT DYEING
         SODIUM ACETATE                      DISPERSE DYEING
    RT   ACETATE ESTERS                      HYDROXYLAMINE
         ACETIC ACID                         METALLIZED DYEING
                                             MORDANT DYEING
ACETIC ACID                                  NEUTRAL DYEING
    BT   CARBOXYLIC ACIDS                    OVERDYEING
         ORGANIC ACIDS                       PIGMENT DYEING
    RT   ACETATE ESTERS                      REACTIVE DYEING
         ACETATE SALTS                       SULFUR DYEING
         ACETIC ANHYDRIDE                    VAT DYEING
         HYDROXYACETIC ACID
         PERACETIC ACID            ACID DYES
                                        NT   MILLING DYES
ACETIC ANHYDRIDE                        BT   ANIONIC DYES
    BT   ACID ANHYDRIDES                      DYES (BY CHEMICAL CLASSES)
    RT   ACETIC ACID                    RT   ACID DYEING
                                             BASIC DYES
ACETONE                                      DYEING (BY DYE CLASSES)
    BT   KETONES                             DYES (BY FIBER CLASSES)
    RT   HYDROXYACETONE                      NEUTRAL DYES
         SOLVENTS
                                    ACID END GROUPS
ACETONITRILE                            NT   CARBOXYL END GROUPS
    BT   NITRILES                            SULFCNIC END GROUPS
                                        BT   END GROUPS
ACETYLATED COTTON                       RT   AMINE END GROUPS
    BT   CHEMICALLY MODIFIED COTTON          DEGREE OF POLYMERIZATION
    RT   ACETATE FIBERS                      MOLECULAR WEIGHT
         ACETYLATION                         POLYMERIZATION
         AMINIZED COTTON
         BENZOYLATED COTTON
```

FIGURE 13. Partial page from *Thesaurus of Textile Terms* showing relation ships among terms. NT's are narrower terms; BT's, broader terms; and RT's, related terms. USE reference indicates term for that concept.

source of keyterms assigned to documents entered in the TITUS system (see D10) of l'Institut Textile de France. The other textile thesaurus is *Textile Technology Terms,* published by the Institute of Textile Technology in 1966 and used to index abstracts in *Textile Technology Digest* (see D46).

Thesauri in related fields include the recently issued *Engineering Index Thesaurus,* which is based on the *Thesaurus of Engineering Terms* published in 1964 by the Engineers Joint Council; *Thesaurus of Engineering and Scientific Terms* (1967), a joint project of the Department of Defense and the Engineers Joint Council; and *Thesaurus of Pulp and Paper Terms,* published by the Pulp and Paper Research Institute of Canada in 1965 and used by *TAPPI* and *Abstract Bulletin of the Institute of Paper Chemistry* (see D1).

No thesaurus has been adopted as a single source by the textile journals which publish keyterms. For example, *Textile Research Journal* selects keyterms from three thesauri: *Thesaurus of Engineering and Scientific Terms, Textile Technology Terms,* and *Thesaurus of Textile Terms. Bulletin de l'Institut Textile de France* uses the French translation of *Thesaurus of Textile Terms,* plus a list of terms the editors have established for concepts not included in the *Thesaurus.* Other journals apparently use still other lists or thesauri as guides in keyterm indexing, and some evidently have no vocabulary control. Consequently, the R&D employee who maintains a personal information retrieval system probably will want to convert the keyterms provided with journal articles into the equivalent terms of the thesaurus or keyterm list he is using.

Using the keyterm card of the Uniterm system and taking advantage of keyterm indexing by some journals, an individual should be able to index a document in a matter of minutes and to retrieve documents from his personal file with little effort.

H1   **BULLETIN DE L'INSTITUT TEXTILE DE FRANCE*** Paris, l'Institut Textile de France, 1947- . Bimonthly. Approximately $25/ year. In French.

French and English keyterms and summaries have been published with each article in the *Bulletin* since January 1968. In addition, keyterms—mots clés—in French (see Figure 11) are listed for each abstract published in the Abstracts section.

Keyterms are chosen primarily from the French translation of *Thesaurus of Textile Terms* (see H34).

Bulletin de l'Institut Textile de France ceased publication at the end of 1971. The reports formerly published in the *Bulletin* now appear in *Bulletin Scientifique de l'Institut Textile de France.* The abstracts which had been published in the *Bulletin* are now being published in *l'Industrie Textile* (Paris, Editions de l'Industrie Textile, 1884- , monthly, approximately $24/year). These abstracts and keyterms selected for the documents are still used as input to the Institut's TITUS system.

H2 **CHEMIEFASERN** Frankfurt, Deutscher Fachverlag, Gmbh, 1919- . Monthly. Approximately $16/year. In German.

English and French abstracts of the articles in each issue are published in a separate section in the front of this journal.

H3 **ENGINEERING INDEX THESAURUS** New York, Engineering Index, 1971. $19.50. From: CCM Information Corporation, 866 Third Ave., New York, N.Y. 10022.

Contains nearly 12,000 terms useful in the fields of plastics and electronics engineering. Based on the Engineers Joint Council *Thesaurus of Engineering Terms* published in 1964, but oriented to the two specific areas mentioned above.

H4 **EUROPEAN POLYMER JOURNAL** Oxford, England, Pergamon, 1965- . Monthly. $100/year.

Articles in this *Journal* usually are written in English or French, and occasionally in German. Abstracts in English, French, German, and Spanish are given for each article—at the beginning of the article in the language in which it was written and following the article in the other three languages.

H5 **FASERFORSCHUNG UND TEXTILTECHNIK** Berlin, Akademie-Verlag Berlin, 1950- . Monthly. Approximately $46/year. In German.

English, German, and Russian abstracts are published at the beginning of each article.

H6 **FIBRE SCIENCE AND TECHNOLOGY** Essex, England, Elsevier Publishing Co. Ltd., 1968- . Quarterly. Approximately $25/year.

The articles in this journal usually are in English, but occasionally are published in French. Summaries in English and the language of the paper, if foreign, are given at the beginning of most articles and in the "Technical Notes" section.

H7   **JOURNAL OF APPLIED POLYMER SCIENCE**   New York, Interscience Publishers, 1959- . Monthly. $150/year.
Each article is preceded by a synopsis in the original language, which is usually English.

H8   **JOURNAL OF MACROMOLECULAR SCIENCE, PART A: CHEMISTRY**   New York, Marcel Dekker, 1967- . Monthly except February, April, June, and September. $85/year.
Summary provided at the beginning of each article.

H9   **JOURNAL OF MACROMOLECULAR SCIENCE, PART B: PHYSICS**
New York, Marcel Dekker, 1967- . Quarterly. $55/year.
A summary precedes each article.

H10   **JOURNAL OF MACROMOLECULAR SCIENCE, PART D: REVIEWS IN POLYMER TECHNOLOGY**   New York, Marcel Dekker, 1971- .
Semiannual. $17.50/year.
An abstract is provided with each review.

H11   **JOURNAL OF POLYMER SCIENCE, PART A-1: POLYMER CHEMISTRY**   New York, Interscience Publishers, 1966- . Monthly.
$325/year, including Parts A-2, B, and C.
Each article is preceded by a synopsis.

H12   **JOURNAL OF POLYMER SCIENCE, PART A-2: POLYMER PHYSICS**   New York, Interscience Publishers, 1966- . Monthly.
$325/year, including Parts A-1, B, and C.
Each article is preceded by a synopsis.

H13   **JOURNAL OF POLYMER SCIENCE, PART C: POLYMER SYMPOSIA**   New York, Interscience Publishers, 1963- . Irregular.
$325/year, including Parts A-1, A-2, and B.
Each article is preceded by a synopsis.

H14 **JOURNAL OF RESEARCH OF THE NATIONAL BUREAU OF STANDARDS, Section A; Physics and Chemistry** Washington, D.C., U.S. Government Printing Office, 1959- . Bimonthly. $9.50/year.

Beginning with the first issue in 1970, an abstract and keywords have been published with each article.

H15 **JOURNAL OF THE SOCIETY OF DYERS AND COLOURISTS** Bradford, England, The Society of Dyers and Colourists, 1884- . Monthly. Approximately $30/year.

An abstract is given at the beginning of each article.

H16 **JOURNAL OF THE TEXTILE INSTITUTE** Manchester, England, The Textile Institute, 1910- . Monthly. Approximately $62/ year, including *Textile Institute and Industry* and *Textile Progress.*

Keyterms and an abstract (see Figure 10) have been provided for each article published in the *Journal* since January 1968. As early as 1950, most articles were abstracted or summarized.

H17 **JOURNAL OF THE TEXTILE MACHINERY SOCIETY OF JAPAN** (English Edition) Osaka, The Textile Machinery Society of Japan, 1955- . Bimonthly. Approximately $9/year.

Contains translations of articles which appeared within the previous year in *Sen-i Kikai Gakkaishi*, the Japanese version of this *Journal*. Each article is preceded by a brief abstract.

Each issue also includes English abstracts of articles published in the most recent previous issues of *Sen-i Gakkaishi* (see H24), *Sen-i Kikai Gakkaishi* (see H25), and *Sen-i Seihin Shohi-Kagaku* (*Journal of the Japan Research Association for Textile End-Uses*).

H18 **KEYTERM LIST** Manchester, England, The Library and Information Department, Shirley Institute, March 1972.

This *List* is used for Shirley Institute's Specialized Textile Information Service. These keyterms are being used, at present, to index documents abstracted in *World Textile Abstracts* (see D51).

The *Keyterm List* is based on the MIT *Thesaurus of Textile Terms* (see H34), although many terms have been added. It contains approximately 9,000 general keyterms and about 1,000 trade names and manufacturer's names printed in a separate section. Both American and British spellings are included for many keyterm entries. Appendixes will be issued periodically until the STI thesaurus is published, probably in 1973.

H19 **MACROMOLECULES** Washington, D.C., American Chemical Society, 1968- . Bimonthly. $12/year to members; $24/year to nonmembers.

Each article is introduced with an abstract.

H20 **MATERIALS RESEARCH AND STANDARDS** Philadelphia, American Society for Testing and Materials, 1961- . Monthly. $8/year.

Keywords have been listed for each article since January 1970. Abstracts also have been provided for most articles since that time.

H21 **MELLIAND TEXTILBERICHTE INTERNATIONAL** Heidelberg, Melliand Textilberichte KG, 1923- . Monthly. Approximately $22/year. In German.

Abstracts of articles in each issue are given in English, French, German, and Spanish in a separate section of the journal.

H22 **POLYMER** Guildford, England, IPC Science and Technology Press Ltd., 1960- . $56/year; $84/year, air-mail.

An abstract precedes each article.

H23 **POLYMER ENGINEERING AND SCIENCE** Manchester, N.H., Society of Plastics Engineers, Inc., 1961- . Bimonthly. $15/year to members; $20/year to nonmembers; $50/year to corporate, institutional, and library subscribers. Each article is preceded by an abstract.

H24 **SEN-I GAKKAISHI (Journal of the Society of Fiber Science and Technology)** Tokyo, Society of Textile and Cellulose Industries, 1944- . Monthly. Approximately $7/year. In Japanese.

English summaries are published with each article. English abstracts of articles in the journal are also published in *Journal of the Textile Machinery Society of Japan* (English Edition) (see H17).

H25 **SEN-I KIKAI GAKKAISHI (Journal of the Textile Machinery Society of Japan)** Osaka, Textile Machinery Society of Japan, 1948- . Approximately $11/year. In Japanese.

English summaries are provided for each article. Articles in this journal are also abstracted in the English-language edition (see H17).

H26 **TAPPI** New York, Technical Association of the Pulp and Paper Industry, 1949- . Monthly. $25/year, including membership.

Keyterms and abstracts have been published with each article since 1966. The source of keyterms for *TAPPI* articles is either *Thesaurus of Pulp and Paper Terms* (see H33) or *Thesaurus of Engineering and Scientific Terms* (see H32), except for those terms identified with asterisks.

H27 **TEXTIL-PRAXIS INTERNATIONAL** Stuttgart, Konradin-Verlag Robert Kohlhammer, 1966- . Monthly. Approximately $24/year. In German.

Summary of articles in each issue published in English, French, German, and Spanish in separate section of the journal.

H28 **TEXTILE CHEMIST AND COLORIST** Research Triangle Park, N.C., American Association of Textile Chemists and Colorists, 1969- . Monthly. $3.75/year to members; $7.50/year to nonmembers.

Abstracts and keyterms have been provided with each article since the first issue. This journal also publishes a cumulative "Key Term Index" in each issue (see Figure 12).

H29 **TEXTILE RESEARCH JOURNAL** Princeton, N.J., Textile Research Institute, 1930- . Monthly. $50/year.

From 1948 to 1969, abstracts were published with each article. Beginning in January 1969, keyterms also have been provided (see Figure 10), which are selected from *Thesaurus of Textile Terms* (see H34), *Textile Technology Terms* (see H30), or *Thesaurus of Engineering and Scientific Terms* (see H32).

H30 **TEXTILE TECHNOLOGY TERMS: An Information Retrieval Thesaurus** By Robert S. Merkel and William C. Harris. Charlottesville, Va., Institute of Textile Technology, 1966. $20.

This thesaurus contains entries for about 6,000 terms and is used in indexing abstracts published in *Textile Technology Digest* (see D46). Second edition in preparation.

H31 **TEXTILVEREDLUNG** Basel, Switzerland, Schweizerisher Verein der Chemiker-Coloristen (SVCC) and Schweizerisher Vereinigung von Farbereifachleuten (SVF), 1966- . Monthly. Approximately $14/year. In German.

English and German summaries are printed with each article.

H32 **THESAURUS OF ENGINEERING AND SCIENTIFIC TERMS** New York, Engineers Joint Council, 1967. $11.50.

A list of engineering and related scientific terms and their relationships for use as a vocabulary reference in indexing and retrieving technical information. Prepared jointly by the Engineers Joint Council and Department of Defense and maintained by the Defense Documentation Center (see E4), this is a major revision of the *Thesaurus of Engineering Terms* published by EJC in 1964.

H33   **THESAURUS OF PULP AND PAPER TERMS**   Pointe Claire, Quebec, Pulp and Paper Research Institute of Canada, 1965. $10. From: Pulp and Paper Research Institute of Canada, Technical Information Division, 570 St. John's Road, Pointe Claire, Quebec, Canada.

Contains about 2,000 terms related to pulp and paper products, processes, uses, and other aspects. Used in keyword indexing by *TAPPI* (see H26) and *Abstract Bulletin of the Institute of Paper Chemistry* (see D1). Second edition in preparation.

H34   **THESAURUS OF TEXTILE TERMS Covering Fibrous Materials and Processes**   Edited by Stanley Backer and Emery I. Valko. 2nd Edition. Cambridge, Mass. (and London), Fibers and Polymers Division, Department of Mechanical Engineering, Massachusetts Institute of Technology, 1969. $25.

This *Thesaurus* was developed under the sponsorship of the U.S. Department of Commerce. It is an integral part of the Textile Information Retrieval Program (TIRP), an interactive computerized system for retrieval of textile information developed at MIT (see D43).

The *Thesaurus* contains about 8,000 terms and has been used as the authority in the development of the Shirley Institute *Keyterm List* (see H18). It has been translated into a number of European languages and Japanese which, eventually, will permit storage of data in a textile information retrieval system in one language and retrieval using any of several other languages.

9

Progress in Textile Information Handling

While the chemical industry has led—mainly through the efforts of the Chemical Abstracts Service of the American Chemical Society—in developing scientific information services in the United States, the textile industry has made some giant strides in information handling during the last decade. The progress made results from work by commercial suppliers of information services, various textile societies, user groups, and projects sponsored by the U.S. Department of Commerce.

One very significant advance was the development of the *Thesaurus of Textile Terms* by Dr. Stanley Backer and his coworkers at MIT under a Department of Commerce contract. The first edition of the *Thesaurus,* developed with suggestions from information scientists experienced in indexing and retrieving textile documents, was published in 1966. The second expanded edition appeared in 1969. Through the efforts of the Commission to Establish a Multi-Language Glossary of the European Group for Exchange of Experience on the Direction of Textile Research and of the Textile Machinery Society of Japan, this *Thesaurus* has now been translated into nine foreign languages. In the near future, a glossary based on these translations will be published in nine versions, each listing the terms in alphabetical order in one language and providing equivalent terms in each of the other languages, with the exception of Japanese. However, an English-Japanese glossary will be included in each of the nine editions. This *Thesaurus* has been adopted as the basic source for keyterm indexing by l'Institut Textile de France and Shirley Institute.

The development of the MIT *Thesaurus* was an essential part[1] of a larger project: to develop and demonstrate an information retrieval system for textile information. A computer-based interactive system was programmed by the MIT team, and approximately 11,000 documents abstracted in *Journal of the Society of Dyers and Colourists* and *Journal of the Textile Institute* were indexed to provide a data base for demonstration of the system's capabilities. The system was successfully demonstrated at the annual meeting of the Textile Research Institute in New York in April 1967. Later, under Commerce Department sponsorship, it was demonstrated in Raleigh, N.C., for small groups of users, by Dr. Robert Work of the School of Textiles of North Carolina State University. Another demonstration was made at North Carolina Science and Technology Research Center for the Textile Information Users Council meeting in May 1970. The information retrieval programs developed at MIT are not being used at present—probably because of the continued high cost for the use of on-line systems—but the data base developed in association with the system is available for batch searching at North Carolina Science and Technology Research Center.

At about the same time that the first edition of the MIT *Thesaurus* became available, the Institute of Textile Technology published *Textile Technology Terms,* the thesaurus used in keyterm indexing of documents abstracted in *Textile Technology Digest.* ITT's thesaurus was produced in conjunction with the development of the industry's first commercial mechanized systems for information retrieval. Since 1966, ITT has offered keyterm entries on punched cards for searching by collator or on magnetic tape for computerized information retrieval. The Institute also has provided, since that time, computer-produced

---

[1] Backer, S., "The Thesaurus as a First Step in an Information-Retrieval System." *Textile Institute and Industry* 5:91-96, 1967.

keyterm indexes in dual dictionary form for manual searching.

The next significant contribution to textile information services came with publication of *World Textile Abstracts* by Shirley Institute. Until 1969, the Institute had published *Shirley Institute Summary of Current Literature*, primarily for internal use, although it was later reprinted in the "Abstracts" section of *Journal of the Textile Institute*. With *World Textile Abstracts*, the Institute has expanded the coverage of its earlier abstract bulletin and, in addition, has developed a magnetic tape data base for computerized information retrieval. It also plans, in the future, to offer computer search programs for the magnetic tapes.

Very recently, l'Institut Textile de France announced the availability of its TITUS system for retrieving textile information. This new service, offered on magnetic tape, is based mainly on keyterm entries for articles and abstracts published since 1968 in *Bulletin de l'Institut Textile de France*. TITUS is designed for use on IBM 360 computers, and information retrieval programs as well as the data base are offered by ITF.

An information service devoted solely to patents also is available to the textile industry. In 1970, Derwent Publications Ltd. began publication of the *Textiles, Paper* section of the *Central Patents Index*, which covers patents from 12 major industrial countries.

As computer-based textile information retrieval systems have evolved, North Carolina Science and Technology Research Center has acquired most of the data bases to provide information services to all parts of the textile industry. In addition to the NASA and DOD files, NCSTRC now has the MIT data base, the data bases for *Textile Technology Digest* and *World Textile Abstracts*, and is considering the possibility of obtaining the TITUS magnetic tapes.

With recognition of the need for information retrieval aids came responsive changes in some of the textile journals. Annual indexes became more common, abstracts with each article began to appear, and English-language abstracts began to be included in a number of foreign journals. Several textile journals now provide keyterms as well as abstracts for each article, with *Textile Chemist and Colorist* and *Journal of the Textile Institute* publishing keyterm indexes, either cumulatively throughout the year or annually.

While these gains were being made, the textile industry also suffered some losses in information media. Several textile journals have disappeared in recent years through mergers. *Natural and Synthetic Fibers,* which published in-depth abstracts including many for articles from German and Japanese journals, ceased publication in 1966. Two journals which were partial translations of their German counterparts, *Melliand Textile Reports* and *Textil-Praxis (International Edition),* also suspended publication during the past decade. However, several new cover-to-cover translations of Russian journals have appeared recently, and *Technology of the Textile Industry U.S.S.R.*—published by the Textile Institute since 1960—and the English edition of the *Journal of the Textile Machinery Society of Japan*—published since 1955—are still in existence.

While there have been significant advances in both the technology and scope of textile information services, deficiencies still do exist, and the needs for certain specialized services are not being fulfilled. With firsthand knowledge of these deficiencies and the determination to overcome them, a group of textile information scientists formed the Textile Information Users Council[2] in May 1969. In essence, the TIUC objectives are to inform the suppliers of textile information services of the needs of U.S. users, to promote the improvement of existing services and the development of new services responsive to the industry, and to act as an advisory board for current and potential suppliers of textile information services.

At its first meeting, the Council formulated a detailed outline of the information services required by the U.S. textile industry and made it a part of the meeting *Proceedings.* This document was sent to major suppliers of such services, accompanied by an invitation to discuss with the Council their capabilities for providing all or some of the recommended services.

Since that time, the TIUC has held semiannual meetings. At several of these meetings, reports of progress in information services have been presented by representatives of the Institute of Textile Technology *(Textile Technology Digest),* Shirley Institute *(World Textile Abstracts),* Derwent Publications Ltd. *(Central Patents Index),* l'Institut Textile de France *(Bulletin de l'Institut Textile de France* and TITUS), Chemical

---

[2] Richardson, R. J. "Taming the Computer." *Modern Textiles Magazine,* 52:41-43, October 1971.

Abstracts Service *(Chemical Abstracts)*, Predicasts, Information Systems Design, Economic Information Systems, and others.

Between these meetings, special committees have made thorough studies of the coverage and speed of publication of the most important textile information services. Currently, they are evaluating the quality of abstracts and indexes. Committee reports have been given at TIUC meetings, included in the *Proceedings,* and transmitted to suppliers of information services for comment. Other committees are determining the need for microfilm editions of textile journals, attempting to find organizations interested in publishing or subsidizing cover-to-cover translations of the more important foreign textile journals, and trying to interest appropriate organizations in providing a service for commercial textile information.

As a direct result of TIUC efforts, Shirley Institute now offers monthly subject indexes to *World Textile Abstracts;* the Ralph McElroy Co. has begun publication of cover-to-cover translations of *Melliand Textilberichte International* and *Textilveredlung;* Robert Merkel of the Institute of Textile Technology has produced, on a one-month experimental basis, *Textile News Index,* which is a weekly index to marketing and commercial information related to the textile industry; and Derwent Publications Ltd. and Shirley Institute are investigating the possible market for their proposed joint production of a computer-readable keyterm index to worldwide textile patents.

The TIUC believes it has been successful in communicating to suppliers the unsatisfied information needs of its members and feels that its efforts already have resulted in improvements in the effectiveness of textile information services. The Council looks forward to continued progress in both quality and timeliness.

The TIUC welcomes new members and reports of existing or potential information services which would be of value to the textile industry. Full participating membership is limited to those who are directly concerned with providing information services within their own organizations. For further information about membership or activities, contact one of the following members of the TIUC steering committee: Mrs. Darlene L. Ball, Manager, Technical Information Services, Burlington Industries, Inc., P.O. Box 21327, Greensboro, N.C. 27420; Miss Joan Gallagher, Head Librarian, Organic Chemicals Division,

American Cyanamid Co., Bound Brook, N.J. 08805; Dr. Erick I. Hoegberg, Head, Technical Information Group, American Viscose Division, FMC, Marcus Hook, Pa. 19103; Mr. Ronald J. Richardson, Manager, Marketing Systems, Fibers Division, Allied Chemical Corp., One Times Square, New York, N.Y. 10036; Miss Helen G. Sommar, Manager, Technical Information Center, Celanese Fibers Co., P.O. Box 1414, Charlotte, N.C. 28201; or Dr. James G. Van Oot, Information Systems Division, E. I. du Pont de Nemours and Co., 3211 Centre Road Building, Wilmington, Del. 19898.

Index

This is an index to (1) titles of publications, (2) names of libraries and other information resources, and (3) subjects covered by (1) and (2). Titles of publications are in italics.

Since documented information appears in many different forms, an attempt has been made to differentiate between the major forms, e.g., books, patents, periodicals, reports, etc. Where the catchall term "literature" is used, it may be taken to include bibliographies, books, conference papers, patents, periodicals, reports, theses, and translations.

Another catchall term used in this index is "key." This denotes, regardless of form (print, cards, magnetic tape, etc.), any means for searching and identifying specific portions of the "literature" by subject, author, or other aspect. "Keys" are distinct from "guides" or the synonymous term "directories" in that "guides" usually describe literature items as a whole, whereas "keys" attempt to provide access to the contents of the literature items. "Guides," of course, may have their own "keys." This index is intended as a "key" to this *Guide*.

WITHDRAWAL